LINES AROUND STAMFORD

including Peterborough, Sleaford, Spalding and Market Harborough

Vic Mitchell and Keith Smith

Front cover: Cross Country DMU no. 170114 is seen on 21st March 2009, surrounded by the architectural joys of Stamford station. (J.Whitehouse)

Back cover: The Railway Clearing House map of 1947 has had the line south of Stamford added, as it had closed in 1929.

ACKNOWLEDGEMENTS

We are very grateful for the assistance received from many of those mentioned in the credits, also from A.J.Castledine, G.Croughton, G.Gartside, S.C.Jenkins, N.Langridge, B.Lewis, J.P.McCrickard, J.Nash, T.Walsh, and in particular our always supportive families.

Published December 2016

ISBN 978 1 908174 98 7

© Middleton Press, 2016

Typesetting & design Cassandra Morgan

Published by
Middleton Press
Easebourne Lane
Midhurst
West Sussex
GU29 9AZ
Tel: 01730 813169
Email: info@middletonpress.co.uk
www.middletonpress.co.uk

Printed and bound by CPI Group (UK) Ltd, Croydon, CR0 4YY

CONTENTS

INDEX

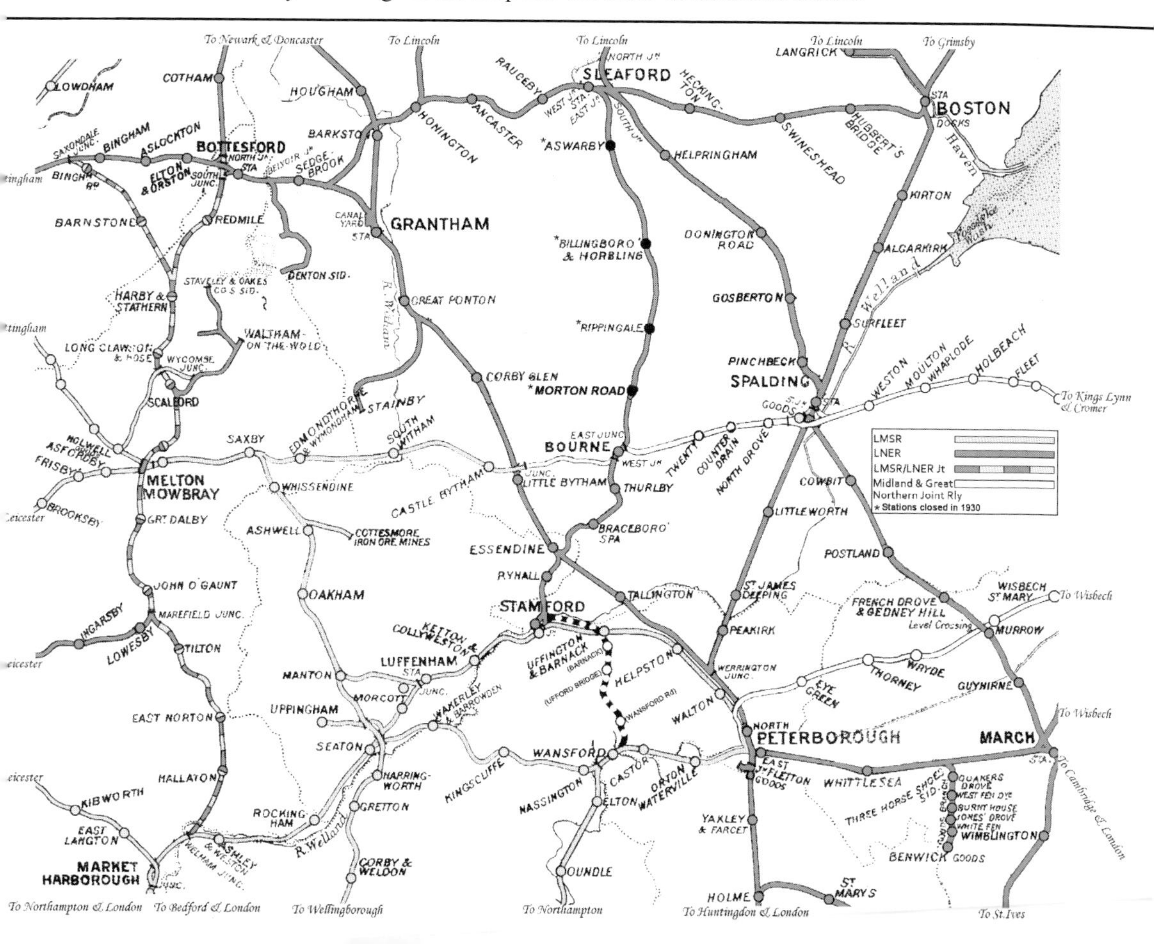

I. The 1947 Railway Clearing House map has the route destinations added.

GEOGRAPHICAL SETTING

1. Market Harborough to Peterborough via Stamford

The first named is a long-established commercial centre in an area largely on limestone and drained by southern tributaries of the River Welland. The route is close to this as it flows northeast to enter The Wash, north of Spalding.

The ground generally slopes down eastwards to the Stamford area, where it merges with the districts known as the Bedford Level and the Soke of Peterborough.

The route began in Northamptonshire, close to its boundary with Leicestershire. It soon ran close to the southern borders of Rutland and then Lincolnshire. It finally entered Cambridgeshire, at Peterborough.

2. Sleaford to Stamford via Bourne

The route southward as far as Bourne is near the foot of the limestone hills, close to the western border of the Fenland. At Bourne, the line rises onto higher ground and later passes over the River Glen as it approaches Stamford.

The route was almost entirely within the county of Lincolnshire.

3. Stamford to Wansford

Initially the line ran east along the Welland Valley, before turning south onto higher ground. Its trains moved from Lincs into Northants as they crossed the river. They ran through Huntingdonshire for a short distance, before they reached Wansford.

4. Spalding to Murrow

The entire route is across Fenland and thus passes over many drains. It initially runs over the River Welland, which was navigable. At French Drove, the line ran from Lincolnshire into Cambridgeshire.

The maps are to the scale of 25ins to 1 mile, with north at the top, unless otherwise indicated.

HISTORICAL BACKGROUND

1. Market Harborough to Peterborough (via Stamford)

The London & North Western Railway reached Market Harborough from Rugby on 1st May 1851 and opened to Rockingham on 1st June of that year. Extension to Luffingham followed on 2nd June 1851. Here it joined the Midland Railway, which had opened between Oakham and Stamford on 1st May 1848. The MR had been running between the latter and Peterborough since 2nd October 1846. The LNWR and the MR became constituents of the London Midland & Scottish Railway in 1923.

2. Sleaford to Stamford (via Bourne)

The Boston, Sleaford & Midland Counties Railway reached Sleaford from Grantham in 1857 and continued east to Boston in 1859. The lines from Sleaford north to Lincoln and southeast to Spalding were in use from 1882. Our route south to Bourne, Essendine and Stamford came into use in stages: on 21st January 1872, 16th May 1860 and 1st November 1856 respectively. At Bourne, it joined the Midland & Eastern Railway of 1866 (from the east) and the Eastern & Midlands Railway of 1893 (from the west). At Essendine, it met the 1852 Great Northern Railway, which ran north-south. There was no through running between the branches.

The line north of Bourne was GNR property from the outset, but south thereof was owned by the Bourn & Essendine Railway until 1864, when the GNR acquired it. (Bourne received an 'e' in 1872.) The Stamford & Essendine Railway became part of the London & North Eastern Railway in 1923, as did the GNR.

3. Stamford to Wansford

The S&ER ran between these places from 6th August 1867 and the company was leased by the GNR from 15th December 1893. The LNER acquired the branch in 1923.

4. Spalding to Murrow

Initially, the route was GNR property and it opened on 2nd September 1867. It was operated jointly with the Great Eastern Railway from 1879 until 1923, when it became part of the LNER. At Murrow, it crossed the 1866 route from Peterborough to Sutton Bridge, which became part of the Midland & Great Northern Railway in 1893 and the LMS & LNER Joint Railway in 1923. The line from Spalding continued south to March in the same ownership. Closure south from Spalding to passengers came on 11th September 1961, but the line remained open for freight and seasonal passenger trains until November 1982.

Nationalisation

This took place in 1948 and the LMSR formed most of the London Midland Region of British Railways, while the LNER largely became its Eastern Region.

Closures to passengers

Stamford to Wansford	1st July 1929
Sleaford to Bourne	22nd September 1930
Bourne to Essendine	18th June 1951
Essendine to Stamford	15th June 1959
Spalding to Murrow	11th September 1961
Market Harborough to Stamford	6th June 1966

Privatisation

The remaining route in use is that between Oakham and Peterborough via Stamford. From 2nd March 1997, the franchise to operate the line went to Central Trains. From 11th November 2007, the service was provided by East Midlands Trains and CrossCountry Trains.

PASSENGER SERVICES

Trains running on at least five weekdays are stated below, with Sunday trains in brackets.

With the east-west route having been realigned southwards and then later having its traffic origins altered in the west, the study of services must be fragmented. The same applies north-south, as there were four different operational lengths connected at one period.

We start in the West. The 1850 timetable showed the LNWR running to Peterborough with four stopping trains and one fast on weekdays (plus one on Sundays). By 1880, the figures were 3 and 2 (1), but trains were direct via the Nene Valley.

From Oakham:

	Weekdays Stopping	Weekdays Express	Sundays (Fast)
1912	5	1	2
1928	7	1	1
1947	6	0	3
1960	6	0	1

By 2000 they were hourly, but few ran on Sunday mornings.

Sleaford to Bourne

In 1873, 5 (0) were on offer and by 1929 it was 4 (0). Closure soon followed.

Bourne to Essendine

The 1865 service was 6 (0); by 1902 it was 8 (0). In 1950, 6 (0) were on offer before closure.

Essendine to Stamford

An early service in 1865 comprised 11 (2) trains. By 1928, it was 12 (0). In 1958, 6 (0).

Stamford to Wansford

The 1867 figures were 5 (0) and in 1903 the offerings were 7 (0), plus one extra on Fridays. 1928 was the final full year and 2 (0) were on offer.

Spalding to Murrow

The 1869 timetable showed 3 (0), with one more, Fridays only. In 1911 we find 5 (0) stopping trains, plus 4 (1) expresses. In 1959, these figures were 1 (0) and 6 (1).

BLISWORTH, NORTHAMPTON, WELLINGBRO', STAMFORD & PETERBORO'—London & North Western.
R. Dockray, Engineer, London and North Western, Southern Division.

Miles fm London	For Stations between London and Blisworth, page 34. Down.	1 2 3 morn	mrn	exp. morn	morn	morn	noon	aft.	aft.	aft.	aft.		Sundays morn	Sundays aft.
	London (Eus.Sq.St) dep	..	6 15	7†15	9 0	10 15	12 0	2 0	4 0	5 30	9‖0	..	7*30	9‖0
	Birmingham..	..	..	7 0	..	10 30	..	..	4 0	5 45	..	..	..	..
	Blisworth (2)........	..	8 44	9 59	10 35	12 33	2 24	4 53	6 10	7 58	11 20	..	10 10	11 20
67¾	**Northampton**	7 0	9 5	10 25	11 5	12 50	3 0	5 20	6 30	8 15	11 40	..	10 35	11 40
71¼	Billing Road........	7 2	..	10 33	..	..	3 2	..	6 38	..	..	..	10 43	..
74¼	Castle Ashby (WhteMill)	7 10	..	10 41	..	..	3 10	..	6 46	..	..	..	10 51	..
78¼	**Wellingborough** ..	7 25	..	10 54	..	1 15	3 25	..	7 0	..	..	..	11 4	..
80¼	Ditchford	7 28	..	..	..	..	3 31	..	..	..	..	..	11 7	..
83	**Higham Ferrars** ..	7 37	..	11 6	..	1 25	3 40	..	7 13	..	..	..	11 16	..
85¾	Ringstead	7 39	..	11 8	..	..	3 42	..	7 15	..	..	..	11 18	..
89	**Thrapston**	7 51	..	11 20	..	1*37	3 54	..	7 30	..	..	..	11 32	..
91¼	Thorpe	7 53	..	11 24	..	..	3 58	..	7 34	..	..	..	11 36	..
94¼	Barnwell	7 57	..	11 28	..	..	4 2	..	7 38	..	..	..	11 40	..
97¼	**Oundle**	8 13	..	11 40	..	1 55	4 14	..	7 54	..	..	..	11 55	..
—	Elton	8 18	..	11 45	..	..	4 19	..	7 59	..	..	..	12 0	..
103¾	**Wansford** ..(Sibson)	8 23	..	11 57	..	2 10	4 31	..	8 11	..	..	..	12 12	..
—	**Stamford**....by coach	9 28	..	12 57	..	3 10	..	..	9 11	..	..	..	1 12	..
—	Castor	8 29	..	..	..	..	4 32	..	..	..	..	..	12 13	..
107¾	Overton..............	8 32	..	12 3	..	..	4 37	..	8 17	..	..	..	12 18	..
110¼	**Peterborough (1)** ..	8 45	..	12 15	..	2 25	4 50	..	8 30	..	..	..	12 30	..

(1) Peterbro' to Boston, Louth, & Hull, p. 85; to Ely, Norwich, and Yarmouth, page 28, and 27.
(1) To St. Ives and Cambridge, page 29.
* A Coach leaves Thrapston at 2 aft. for Cambridge.
† Third class attached to this train from London to Stations, between Northampton and Peterborough.
‡ Third class as far as Blisworth only.
‖ Express mail mixed.
All the Trains between Northampton and Peterborough are Mixed.

March 1850

BOURNE and ESSENDINE.—Great Northern.

Fm South 82; *North* 85; *Essendine* 83.	1&2 e	1,2,3 mrn	1,2,3 mrn	1&2 c	1&2 aft	1,2,3 aft	1&2 aft	1&2 aft	1&2 aft	
Essendine dep	7 15	9 5	1110	1216	2 42	5 5	5 53	7 10	8 10	..
Braceboro' Spa **a**	..	..	..	..	..	**d**	..	..	..	..
Thurlby	7 29	9 19	1124	1230	2 56	..	6 7	7 24	8 24	..
Bourne....arr	7 35	9 25	1130	1236	3 2	5 20	6 15	7 30	8 30	..

Up.	1&2 e	1,2,3 mrn	1&2 b	1&2 c	1&2 aft	1,2,3 aft	1&2 aft	1&2 aft	1&2 aft
Bourne ..dep	6 45	8 20	10 0	1140	1255	4 30	5 25	6 35	7 40
Thurlby	6 51	8 26	10 6	1146	1 1	4 36	..	6 41	7 46
Bracebore' Spa **a**	..	..	..	..	..	..	**d**	..	..
Essndn 85, 82	7 7	8 42	1022	12 2	1 17	4 52	5 40	6 57	8 2

a Braceboro' Spa.—Stop by signal to take up, and set down on informing the Guard at the preceding station.
b 3rd class to the North. **c** On Thursdays and Saturdays only. **d** Do not stop at Braceboro' Spa. **e** On Mondays only

November 1865

BOURNE and SLEAFORD.

Miles	Down.	Week Days only. mrn		mrn		mrn		aft	aft (Saturdays only.)
	London (K.C.) ......dep.	5 5	....	7 15	....	1130	....	3 0	5 45
	Bourne..................dep.	9 5	....	10 55	....	3 10	....	5 55	9 0
2¾	Morton Road................	9 11	....	11 1	....	3 19	....	6 1	9 5
5¼	Rippingale..................	9 17	....	11 7	....	3 28	....	6 7	9 11
9¼	Billingboro' and Horbling..	9 25	....	11 15	....	3 38	....	6 15	9 19
13¾	Aswarby and Scredington ..	9 34	....	11 24	....	3 49	....	6 24	9 29
17½	Sleaford 892, 893, 894 arr.	9 40	....	11 30	....	4 0	....	6 30	9 37

Miles	Up.	Week Days only. mrn (Except Mondays)	mrn (Mondays only.)	mrn		aft (Except Mondays)	aft (Mondays only.)	aft	aft (Saturdays only.)
	Sleaford...............dep.	8 20	8 20	10 13	....	1 48	2 15	4 22	7 55
3½	Aswarby and Scredington...	8 27	8 27	10 20	....	1 55	2 22	4 29	8 2
8	Billingboro' and Horbling...	8 37	8 39	10 29	....	2 5	2 32	4 39	8 12
11¾	Rippingale..................	8 44	8 46	10 35	....	2 12	2 39	4 46	8 19
14¾	Morton Road................	8 55	8 57	10 40	....	2 18	2 45	4 52	8 25
17½	Bourne 1080, 1081, *above* arr.	9 0	9 2	10 45	....	2 28	2 51	4 57	8 30
112½	London (K.C.) ...... arr.	1230	1230	3 55	....	7 0	7 0	9 2	....

August 1928

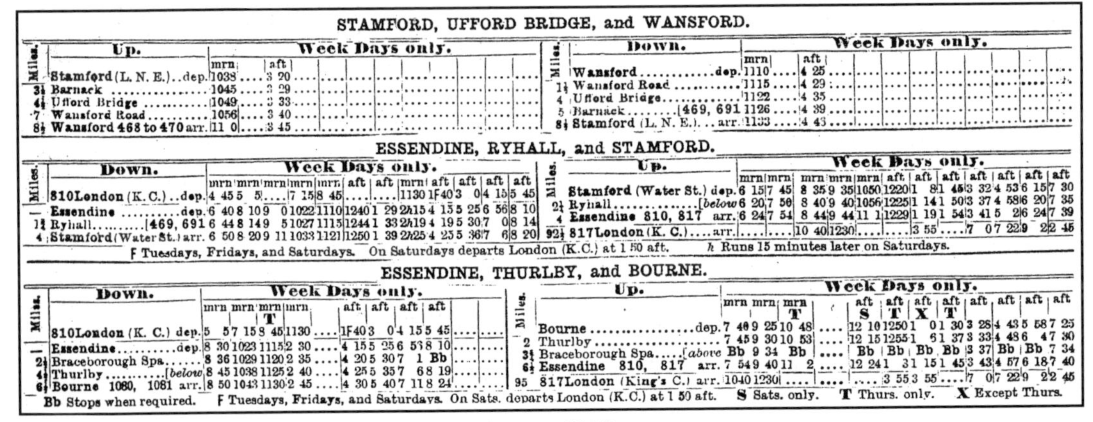

STAMFORD, UFFORD BRIDGE, and WANSFORD.

Miles.	Up.	Week Days only. mrn		aft
	Stamford (L. N. E.)..dep.	1038	....	3 20
3¼	Barnack	1045	....	3 29
4¼	Ufford Bridge	1049	....	3 33
7	Wansford Road	1056	....	3 40
8½	Wansford 468 to 470 arr.	11 0	....	3 45

Miles.	Down.	Week Days only. mrn		aft
	Wansford ....dep.	1110	....	4 25
1¼	Wansford Road	1115	....	4 29
4	Ufford Bridge............	1122	....	4 35
5	Barnack.......[469, 691	1126	....	4 39
8¼	Stamford (L. N. E.)... arr.	1133	....	4 43

ESSENDINE, RYHALL, and STAMFORD.

Miles.	Down.	mrn	mrn	mrn	mrn	mrn	aft	aft	mrn	aft	aft	aft	aft
	810 London (K.C.)..dep.	4 45	5 5	....	7 15	8 45	....	....	1130	1F40	3 0	4 15	5 45
—	Essendine ....dep.	6 40	8 10	9 0	1022	1110	1240	1 29	2h15	4 15	5 25	6 56	8 10
1¾	Ryhall.........[469, 691	6 44	8 14	9 5	1027	1115	1244	1 33	2h19	4 19	5 30	7 0	8 14
4	Stamford (Water St.) arr.	6 50	8 20	9 11	1033	1121	1250	1 39	2h25	4 25	5 36	7 6	8 20

Miles.	Up.	mrn	mrn	mrn	mrn	mrn	aft	aft	aft	aft	aft	aft	aft
	Stamford (Water St.) dep.	6 15	7 45	8 35	9 35	1050	1220	1 8	1 45	3 32	4 53	6 15	7 30
2¼	Ryhall..............[below	6 20	7 50	8 40	9 40	1056	1225	1 14	1 50	3 37	4 58	6 20	7 35
4	Essendine 810, 817 arr.	6 24	7 54	8 44	9 44	11 1	1229	1 19	1 54	3 41	5 2	6 24	7 39
92¼	817 London (K. C.)....arr.	....	....	10 40	1230	....	....	3 55	....	7 0	7 22	9 2	2 45

F Tuesdays, Fridays, and Saturdays. On Saturdays departs London (K.C.) at 1 50 aft. *h* Runs 15 minutes later on Saturdays.

ESSENDINE, THURLBY, and BOURNE.

Miles.	Down.	mrn	mrn	mrn T	mrn		aft	aft	aft	aft		
	810 London (K. C.) dep.	5 5	7 15	8 45	1130	....	1F40	3 0	4 15	5 45	....	....
—	Essendine..........dep.	8 30	1023	1115	2 30	....	4 15	5 25	6 53	8 10	....	....
2¼	Braceborough Spa......	8 36	1029	1120	2 35	....	4 20	5 30	7 1	Bb	....	....
4¼	Thurlby..........[below	8 45	1038	1125	2 40	....	4 25	5 35	7 6	8 19	....	....
6¾	Bourne 1080, 1081 arr.	8 50	1043	1130	2 45	....	4 30	5 40	7 11	8 24	....	....

Miles.	Up.	mrn	mrn	mrn T		aft S	aft T	aft X	aft T	aft	aft	aft	aft
	Bourne ....dep.	7 40	9 25	10 48	....	12 10	1250	1 0	1 30	3 28	4 43	5 58	7 25
2	Thurlby	7 45	9 30	10 53	....	12 15	1255	1 6	1 37	3 33	4 48	6 4	7 30
3¾	Braceborough Spa.....[above	Bb	9 34	Bb	....	Bb	Bb	Bb	Bb	3 37	Bb	Bb	7 34
6¾	Essendine 810, 817 arr.	7 54	9 40	11 2	....	12 24	1 3	1 15	1 45	3 43	4 57	6 18	7 40
95	817 London (King's C.) arr.	1040	1230	....	....	....	3 55	3 55	....	7 0	7 22	9 2	2 45

Bb Stops when required. F Tuesdays, Fridays, and Saturdays. On Sats. departs London (K.C.) at 1 50 aft. S Sats. only. T Thurs. only. X Except Thurs.

August 1928

LEICESTER, SYSTON, MELTON MOWBRAY, STAMFORD, and PETERBRO'.

Week Days.

Miles from Leicester	Station	mrn	mrn	mrn	mrn Except Saturdays.	mrn Through Train, Birmingham to Peterborough.	mrn	mrn	mrn Express to Sheringham, Cromer, Norwich, Yarmouth, and Lowestoft.—Through Carriages, Birmingham to Yarmouth and Lowestoft. Mondays, Fridays, and Saturdays.	mrn	aft Saturdays only.		mrn Through Train, Birmingham to Peterborough.
	642London (St. Pancras)..dep.	2 25	....	4 25	....	....	....	....	8 25	9 50	....	....	10e25
	649Liverpool (Central) .. "	10H35	....	....	....	....	....	5 5	....	8V10	....	....	8 30
	649Manchester (Central). "	12H0	....	....	....	....	....	7 20	....	7F24	....	....	9 55
	689Birmingham (New St.) "	....	4L15	4L15	....	7 30	....	....	9 35	9 35	....	....	11 48
—	Leicester (London Road)..dep.	6 35	....	7 40	8 0	9 6	....	....	1045	1152	....	....	1 0
¾	Humberstone Road	6 38	....	....	8 3	9 9	....	....	....	1155	....	....	....
—	649Nottingham ....dep.	4J30	....	5 56	7J0	7 18	....	....	9J28	1048	....	....	11J50
4¾	Syston	6 45	....	7 48	8 10	9 17	....	....	1055	12 4	....	....	1 7
8	Rearsby	6 55	....	....	8 19	....	....	....	....	1212	....	....	1 16
9	Brooksby	7 1	....	7s55	8 23	9 28	....	....	....	1218	....	....	1 21
11	Frisby	7 7	....	....	8 28	9Z32	....	....	....	1223	....	....	Yy
12¼	Asfordby	7 11	....	....	8 32	9 36	....	....	....	1227	....	....	Ss
—	692Nottingham ....dep.	....	6 45	6 45	7 45	8 35	....	10 25	1038	1124	....	....	12 35
15	Melton Mowbray (Mid.)	7 18	7 38	8 3	8 40	9 43	....	10 53	1010	1234	....	....	1 33
18¾	Saxby 1080	....	7 46	....	8 48	9 54	....	....	1125	1244	....	....	1 43
36¾	1080Bourne ....arr.	....	....	....		1045	....	....	12 2	....		....	2 34
114	1080Sheringham ...... "	....	....	1h11		4Y33	....	4r33	2 34	....		....	....
117¾	1080Cromer (Beach)...... "	....	....	1h23		4Y47	....	4r47	2 47	....		....	....
124	1080Norwich (City) ...... "	....	....	1h25		5Y0	....	5r0	5 0	....		....	....
144½	1080Yarmouth (Beach).... "	....	....	2h5		6Y5	....	6rU5	3 26	....		....	....
156¾	1080Lowestoft (Central) .. "	....	....	2h49		6Y48	....	6rU48	4 5	....		....	....
21	Whissendine	....	7 52	....		....	....	....		1251		....	....
23½	Ashwell	....	7 59	....		10 5	....	....		1257		....	1 53
26½	Oakham	....	8 6	8 23		1012	11 0	....		1 5		....	2 0
—	693London (St. Pan.) A ..dep.	....	....	....	....	8 25	....	....		....		....	....
30	Manton, for Uppingham	....	8 15	8 30	....	1022	11 7	11 20		1 14	....	....	2 7
34	Luffenham 469	....	....	8 38	....	1029	....	....		....	....	....	2 14
36½	Ketton	....	....	8 44	....	1035	....	....		....	....	....	2 20
40	Stamford 886	....	....	8 51	....	1041	....	11 34		....	1 50	....	2 27
42¾	Uffington and Barnack	....	....	8 58	....	1048	....	....		....	1 57	....	2 35
46½	Helpston	....	....	9 5	....	1056	....	....		....	2 5	....	2 43
49¾	Walton (880, 1080	....	....	9 12	....	....	....	....		....	2 12	....	2 50
52	Peterbro' (North) 810, 817,	....	....	9 22	....	11 8	....	11 54		....	2 20	....	3 1
52¾	" (East) ....arr.	....	....	9 28	....	1114	....	11 59		....	2 25	....	3 8
136	860Norwich (Thorpe) ....arr.	....	....	....	....	3 19	....	3 19		....	....	....	5 41
160	860Cromer .... "	....	....	....	....	4 22	....	4 22		....	....	....	6 45
159½	860Lowestoft (Central).. "	....	....	....	....	4 10	....	4 10		....	....	....	6 53
156½	860Yarmouth (Vauxhall) "	....	....	....	....	4 37	....	4 37		....	....	....	6 41
97	880Cambridge 879 ...... "	....	....	....	....	2 9	....	2 9		....	....	....	5 19

Miles from Leicester	Station	aft Through Carriages, Gloucester, Birmingham, Leicester, and Nottingham to Cromer, Norwich, Yarmouth, and Lowestoft, see pages 661, 689, and 1080.	aft	aft Through Train, Nottingham to Bourne, see page 1080.	aft	aft	aft	aft	aft Through Train, Nottingham to Bourne, see page 1080.	aft Through Train, Birmingham to Peterborough.	aft Saturdays only.	Sundays. ngt. Through Train, Birmingham to Peterborough.	Sundays. aft Through Train, Birmingham to Peterborough.
	642London (St. Pancras)..dep.	1225	12 25	....	2 25	....	3 30	4B55	....	6 25	6 30	12 5	3 15
	649Liverpool (Central) .. "	1125	11 25	....	1255	1255	....	3B30	....	4 55	6 25	10T35	3 45
	649Manchester (Central). "	1220	12 20	....	1 45	1 45	....	4B35	....	5 50	7 25	12T0	5 20
	689Birmingham (New St.) "	1 52	1 52	....	2 25	....	4 55	5 15	....	7 18	....	6 55	5 42
—	Leicester (London Road)..dep.	3 22	3 25	....	5 0	5 10	6 13	7 25	....	9 7	1040	9 20	8 0
¾	Humberstone Road	....	....	....	....	5 13	6 16	7 28	....	....	....	9 23	8 3
—	649Nottingham ....dep.	1J25	2 27	....	....	3J52	5J8	5 38	....	7 52	9 35	8J5	6J17
4¾	Syston	3A30	3 35	....	....	5 21	6 24	7 36	....	9 15	1048	9 31	8 11
8	Rearsby	....	3 44	....	....	5 29	6 32	7 44	....	9 22	1057	9 40	8 20
9	Brooksby	....	3 48	....	....	5 33	6 36	7 48	....	9 26	11 2	9 45	8 25
11	Frisby	....	3 53	....	....	5 38	6 41	7 53	....	9 31	....	9 51	8 30
12¼	Asfordby	....	3 57	....	....	5 44	6 45	7 57	....	9 35	1110	9 55	8 34
—	692Nottingham ....dep.	3 12	3 12	4 15	4 15	....	5 48	....	7 25	8 52	....	....	6 43
15	Melton Mowbray (Mid.)	3 50	4 3	5 2	5 22	5 49	6 50	8 2	8 12	9 41	1115	10 2	8 42
18¾	Saxby 1080	4 3	4 12	5 11	5 30	....	7 0	┘	8 22	9 50	....	10 12	8 51
36¾	1080Bourne ....arr.	4 35	....	5 49	....	....	....	....	9 3	....		....	....
114	1080Sheringham ...... "	7 1	....		....	....	....	....		....		....	....
117¾	1080Cromer (Beach)...... "	7 15	....		....	....	....	....		....		....	....
124	1080Norwich (City) ...... "	7 15	....		....	....	....	....		....		....	....
144½	1080Yarmouth (Beach).... "	7 46	....		....	....	....	....		....		....	....
156¾	1080Lowestoft (Central) .. "	8 24	....		....	....	....	....		....		....	....
21	Whissendine	....	4 18		5 37	....	....	....		9 57		....	....
23½	Ashwell	....	4 24		5 43	....	....	....		10 3		10 25	9 4
26½	Oakham	....	4 30		5 50	....	7 13	....		1010		10 32	9 12
—	693London (St. Pan.) A ..dep.	....	....		3 30	....	5 0	....		....	....	....	....
30	Manton, for Uppingham	....	4 40		5 58	....	7 20	....		1018	....	10 42	9 21
34	Luffenham 469	....	4 49		6 6	....	7 27	....		1027	....	10 51	9 30
36½	Ketton	....	4 55		6 12	....	7 33	....		1033	....	10 57	9 38
40	Stamford 886	....	5 1		6 18	....	7 40	....		1040	....	11 5	9 46
42¾	Uffington and Barnack	....	5 8		....	....	....	....		....	....	....	....
46½	Helpston	....	5 16		6 32	....	7 54	....		....	....	11 22	10 0
49¾	Walton (880, 1080	....	5 22		....	....	....	....		....	....	....	10N8
52	Peterbro' (North) 810, 817,	....	5 31		6 42	....	8 8	....		11 0	....	11 33	1015
52¾	" (East) ....arr.	....	5 35		6 49	....	8 13	....		11 5	....	11 40	1021
136	860Norwich (Thorpe) ....arr.	....	9 38	....	1029	....	1 58	....	....	....	....	7 28	1 55
160	860Cromer .... "	....	....	....	....	....	....	....	....	....	....	10 7	....
159½	860Lowestoft (Central).. "	....	10 50	....	....	....	....	....	....	....	....	8 43	....
156½	860Yarmouth (Vauxhall) "	....	10 36	....	1142	....	3 0	....	....	....	....	8 39	3 0
97	880Cambridge 879 ...... "	....	8 3	....	10K5	....	1245	....	....	....	....	4 51	1245

A Via Gretton. A Stops to take up.
B Departs London (St. Pancras) at 4 25, Liverpool (C.) at 2 30, and Manchester (C.) at 3 25 aft. on Sats.
e Except Saturdays.
F Passengers for stations Melton Mowbray to Manton inclusive depart Manchester (Cen.) at 8 55 mrn.
H Departs Liverpool at 9 10 and Manchester (Cen.) 10 40 aft. on Sundays.
h Via Peterboro'. Arrives Sheringham 1 59, Cromer 2 16, Norwich 2 20, Yarmouth 3 6, and Lowestoft at 4 5 aft. on Saturdays.
J Via Leicester.
K Arrives at 9 25 aft. on Saturdays.
L Except Mondays. Via Derby.
N Stops when required to set down.
P Lowestoft (North).
r Via Peterbro'.
Ss Stops at Asfordby on Saturdays.
s Saturdays only.
T Saturday night.
U Arrives Yarmouth (Beach) at 5 17, and Lowestoft (Cen.) at 5 34 aft. on Mondays, Fridays, and Saturdays.
V Via Melton Mowbray.
Y Except Mondays, Fridays, and Saturdays.
Yy Calls at Frisby on Thurs. and Sats.
Z Tuesdays and Saturdays.

August 1928

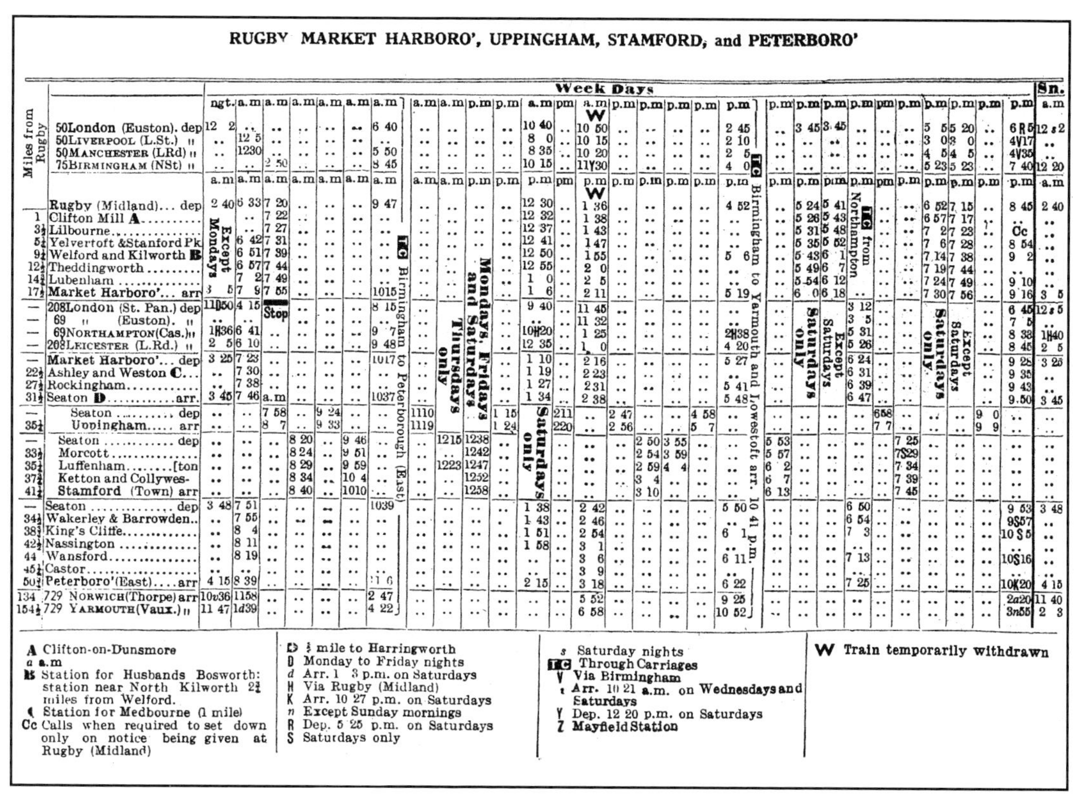

RUGBY MARKET HARBORO', UPPINGHAM, STAMFORD, and PETERBORO'

Week Days

Miles from Rugby	Station	ngt. / a.m Except Mondays	a.m / a.m	a.m / a.m	a.m	a.m	a.m	a.m TC Birmingham to Peterborough (East)	a.m	a.m Thursdays only	p.m Mondays, Fridays and Saturdays	p.m	a.m / p.m Saturdays only	pm	a.m W / p.m W	p.m
	50London (Euston). dep	12 2	..	..	..	..	..	6 40	..	..	..	..	10 40	..	10 50	..
	50Liverpool (L.St.) "	..	12 5	..	..	..	..	..	..	..	..	..	8 0	..	10 15	..
	50Manchester (LRd) "	..	1230	..	..	..	..	5 50	..	..	..	..	8 35	..	10 20	..
	75Birmingham (NSt) "	..	..	2 50	..	..	..	8 45	..	..	..	..	10 15	..	11Y30	..
	Rugby (Midland)... dep	2 40	6 33	7 20	..	..	..	9 47	..	..	..	..	12 30	..	1 36	..
1	Clifton Mill A		..	7 22	..	..	..	..	..	..	..	..	12 32	..	1 38	..
3½	Lilbourne		..	7 27	..	..	..	..	..	..	..	..	12 37	..	1 43	..
5½	Yelvertoft &Stanford Pk		6 42	7 31	..	..	..	..	..	..	..	..	12 41	..	1 47	..
9½	Welford and Kilworth B		6 51	7 39	..	..	..	..	..	..	..	..	12 50	..	1 55	..
12½	Theddingworth		6 57	7 44	..	..	..	..	..	..	..	..	12 55	..	2 0	..
14½	Lubenham		7 2	7 49	..	..	..	..	..	..	..	..	1 0	..	2 5	..
17½	Market Harboro'... arr	3 5	7 9	7 55	..	..	..	1015	..	..	..	..	1 6	..	2 11	..
—	208London (St. Pan.) dep	11D50	4 15	Stop	..	..	..	8 15	..	..	..	..	9 40	..	11 45	..
—	69 " (Euston). "	..	..		..	..	..	..	..	..	..	..	..	..	11 32	..
—	69Northampton(Cas.) "	1H36	6 41	..	..	..	..	9 7	..	..	..	..	10H20	..	1 25	..
—	208Leicester (L.Rd.) "	2 5	6 10	..	..	..	..	9 48	..	..	..	..	12 35	..	1 0	..
—	Market Harboro'... dep	3 25	7 23	..	..	..	..	1017	..	..	..	..	1 10	..	2 16	..
22½	Ashley and Weston C	..	7 30	..	..	..	..	..	..	..	..	..	1 19	..	2 23	..
27½	Rockingham	..	7 38	..	..	..	..	..	..	..	..	..	1 27	..	2 31	..
31½	Seaton D ....arr.	3 45	7 46	a.m	..	..	..	1037	..	..	..	..	1 34	..	2 38	..
—	Seaton .... dep	..	..	7 58	..	9 24	..	..	1110	..	..	1 15		211	..	2 47
35½	Uppingham..... arr	..	..	8 7	..	9 33	..	..	1119	..	..	1 24		220	..	2 56
—	Seaton .... dep	..	..	..	8 20	..	9 46	..	..	1215	1238	..		..	..	..
33½	Morcott	..	..	..	8 24	..	9 51	..	..	..	1242	..		..	..	..
35½	Luffenham........[ton	..	..	..	8 29	..	9 59	..	..	1223	1247	..		..	..	..
37¾	Ketton and Collywes-	..	..	..	8 34	..	10 4	..	..	..	1252	..		..	..	..
41½	Stamford (Town) arr	..	..	..	8 40	..	1010	..	..	..	1258	..		..	..	..
—	Seaton .... dep	3 48	7 51	..	..	..	..	1039	..	..	..	..	1 38	..	2 42	..
34½	Wakerley & Barrowden..	..	7 55	..	..	..	..	..	..	..	..	..	1 43	..	2 46	..
38¾	King's Cliffe	..	8 4	..	..	..	..	..	..	..	..	..	1 51	..	2 54	..
42½	Nassington	..	8 11	..	..	..	..	..	..	..	..	..	1 58	..	3 1	..
44	Wansford	..	8 19	..	..	..	..	..	..	..	..	..	..	..	3 6	..
45¼	Castor	..	..	..	..	..	..	..	..	..	..	..	..	..	3 9	..
50¾	Peterboro'(East)....arr	4 15	8 39	..	..	..	..	11 6	..	..	..	..	2 15	..	3 18	..
134	729 Norwich(Thorpe) arr	10t36	1158	..	..	..	..	2 47	..	..	..	..	..	..	5 52	..
154½	729 Yarmouth(Vaux.) "	11 47	1d39	..	..	..	..	4 22	..	..	..	..	..	..	6 58	..

Miles from Rugby	Station	p.m	p.m	p.m	p.m TC Birmingham to Yarmouth and Lowestoft arr. 10 41 p.m.	p.m	p.m Saturdays only	p.m Except Saturdays	p.m TC from Northampton	pm	p.m	p.m Saturdays only	p.m Except Saturdays	p.m	p.m	Sn. a.m
	50London (Euston). dep	..	..	..	2 45	..	3 45	3 45	..	..	..	5 5	5 20	..	6R5	12s2
	50Liverpool (L.St.) "	..	..	..	2 10	..	..	..	..	..	..	3 0	3 0	..	4V17	..
	50Manchester (LRd) "	..	..	..	2 5	..	..	..	..	..	..	4 5	4 5	..	4V35	..
	75Birmingham (NSt) "	..	..	..	4 0	..	..	..	..	..	..	5 23	5 23	..	7 40	12 20
	Rugby (Midland)... dep	..	..	..	4 52	..	5 24	5 41		..	..	6 52	7 15	..	8 45	2 40
1	Clifton Mill A	..	..	..	..	..	5 26	5 43		..	..	6 57	7 17	..	..	..
3½	Lilbourne	..	..	..	..	..	5 31	5 48		..	..	7 2	7 23	..	Cc	..
5½	Yelvertoft &Stanford Pk	..	..	..	..	..	5 35	5 52		..	..	7 6	7 28	..	8 54	..
9½	Welford and Kilworth B	..	..	..	5 6	..	5 43	6 1		..	..	7 14	7 38	..	9 2	..
12½	Theddingworth	..	..	..	..	..	5 49	6 7		..	..	7 19	7 44	..	..	..
14½	Lubenham	..	..	..	..	..	5 54	6 12		..	..	7 24	7 49	..	9 10	..
17½	Market Harboro'... arr	..	..	..	5 19	..	6 0	6 18	..	..	..	7 30	7 56	..	9 16	3 5
—	208London (St. Pan.) dep	..	..	..	..	..			3 12	..	..			..	6 45	12s5
—	69 " (Euston). "	..	..	..	..	..			3 5	..	..			..	7 5	..
—	69Northampton(Cas.) "	..	..	..	2H38	..			5 31	..	..			..	8 33	1H40
—	208Leicester (L.Rd.) "	..	..	..	4 20	..			5 26	..	..			..	8 45	2 5
—	Market Harboro'... dep	..	..	..	5 27	..			6 24	..	..			..	9 28	3 25
22½	Ashley and Weston C	..	..	..	..	..			6 31	..	..			..	9 35	..
27½	Rockingham	..	..	..	5 41	..			6 39	..	..			..	9 43	..
31½	Seaton D ....arr.	..	..	..	5 48	..			6 47	..	..			..	9.50	3 45
—	Seaton .... dep	..	..	4 58	..	..	..	..	..	658	..	..	..	9 0	..	..
35½	Uppingham..... arr	..	..	5 7	..	..	..	..	..	7 7	..	..	..	9 9	..	..
—	Seaton .... dep	2 50	3 55	..	..	5 53	..	..	..	..	7 25	..	..	..	..	..
33½	Morcott	2 54	3 59	..	..	5 57	..	..	..	..	7S29	..	..	..	..	..
35½	Luffenham........[ton	2 59	4 4	..	..	6 2	..	..	..	..	7 34	..	..	..	..	..
37¾	Ketton and Collywes-	3 4	..	..	..	6 7	..	..	..	..	7 39	..	..	..	..	..
41½	Stamford (Town) arr	3 10	..	..	..	6 13	..	..	..	..	7 45	..	..	..	..	..
—	Seaton .... dep	..	..	..	5 50	..	..	..	6 50	..	..	..	..	..	9 53	3 48
34½	Wakerley & Barrowden..	..	..	..	..	..	..	..	6 54	..	..	..	..	..	9S57	..
38¾	King's Cliffe	..	..	..	6 1	..	..	..	7 3	..	..	..	..	..	10S5	..
42½	Nassington	..	..	..	..	..	..	..	..	..	..	..	..	..	..	..
44	Wansford	..	..	..	6 11	..	..	..	7 13	..	..	..	..	..	10S16	..
45¼	Castor	..	..	..	..	..	..	..	..	..	..	..	..	..	..	..
50¾	Peterboro'(East)....arr	..	..	..	6 22	..	..	..	7 25	..	..	..	..	..	10K20	4 15
134	729 Norwich(Thorpe) arr	..	..	..	9 25	..	..	..	..	..	..	..	..	..	2a20	11 40
154½	729 Yarmouth(Vaux.) "	..	..	..	10 52	..	..	..	..	..	..	..	..	..	3n55	2 3

A Clifton-on-Dunsmore
a a.m
B Station for Husbands Bosworth: station near North Kilworth 2¼ miles from Welford.
C Station for Medbourne (1 mile)
Cc Calls when required to set down only on notice being given at Rugby (Midland)
D ¾ mile to Harringworth
D Monday to Friday nights
d Arr. 1 3 p.m. on Saturdays
H Via Rugby (Midland)
K Arr. 10 27 p.m. on Saturdays
n Except Sunday mornings
R Dep. 5 25 p.m. on Saturdays
S Saturdays only
s Saturday nights
TC Through Carriages
V Via Birmingham
t Arr. 10 21 a.m. on Wednesdays and Saturdays
Y Dep. 12 20 p.m. on Saturdays
Z Mayfield Station
W Train temporarily withdrawn

March 1951

1. Market Harborough to Peterborough

MARKET HARBOROUGH

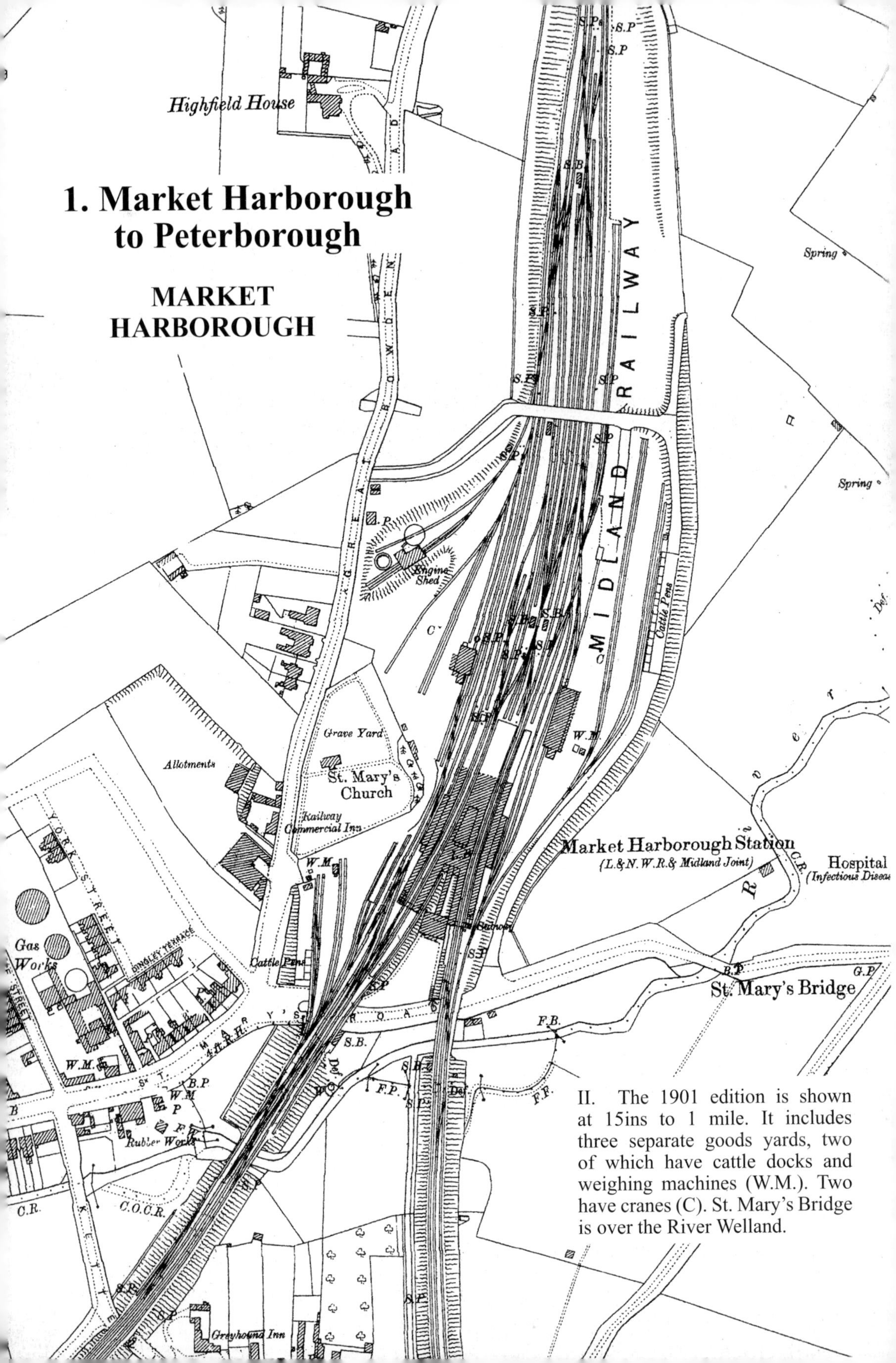

II. The 1901 edition is shown at 15ins to 1 mile. It includes three separate goods yards, two of which have cattle docks and weighing machines (W.M.). Two have cranes (C). St. Mary's Bridge is over the River Welland.

1. The first station was an LNWR creation, but this one was a joint venture with the MR and it opened on 15th February 1886. The population grew to 4400 by 1901 and to 12,020 by 1961. (Milepost 92½)

For other views, see *Market Harborough to Newark* (picures 1 to 9) and *Wellingborough to Leicester* (pictures 39 to 49). Also see the former's map III.

2. The LMS introduced 33 Beyer-Garratts in 1927-30. Each weighed about 155½ tons and were 2-6-6-2s, articulated with a water tank at both ends. This one is southbound in about 1948. (Milepost 92½)

3. Seen from the north end of the same platform on 17th April 1961 is class 5 4-6-0 no. 45407, heading the 2.57pm Leicester to Kettering stopping train. It is close to North Box, which had 55 levers and was in use from 1931 to 29th June 1968, when Leicester Signalling Centre took over the district. (Milepost 92½)

4. The engine shed is on the left of map II and it was coded 15F in 1958-60. It was a sub-shed of Leicester until closure in 1965, when it is seen with class 4F 0-6-0 no. 44529 out of use. The nearby roof was formed by a water tank. (R.S.Carpenter coll.)

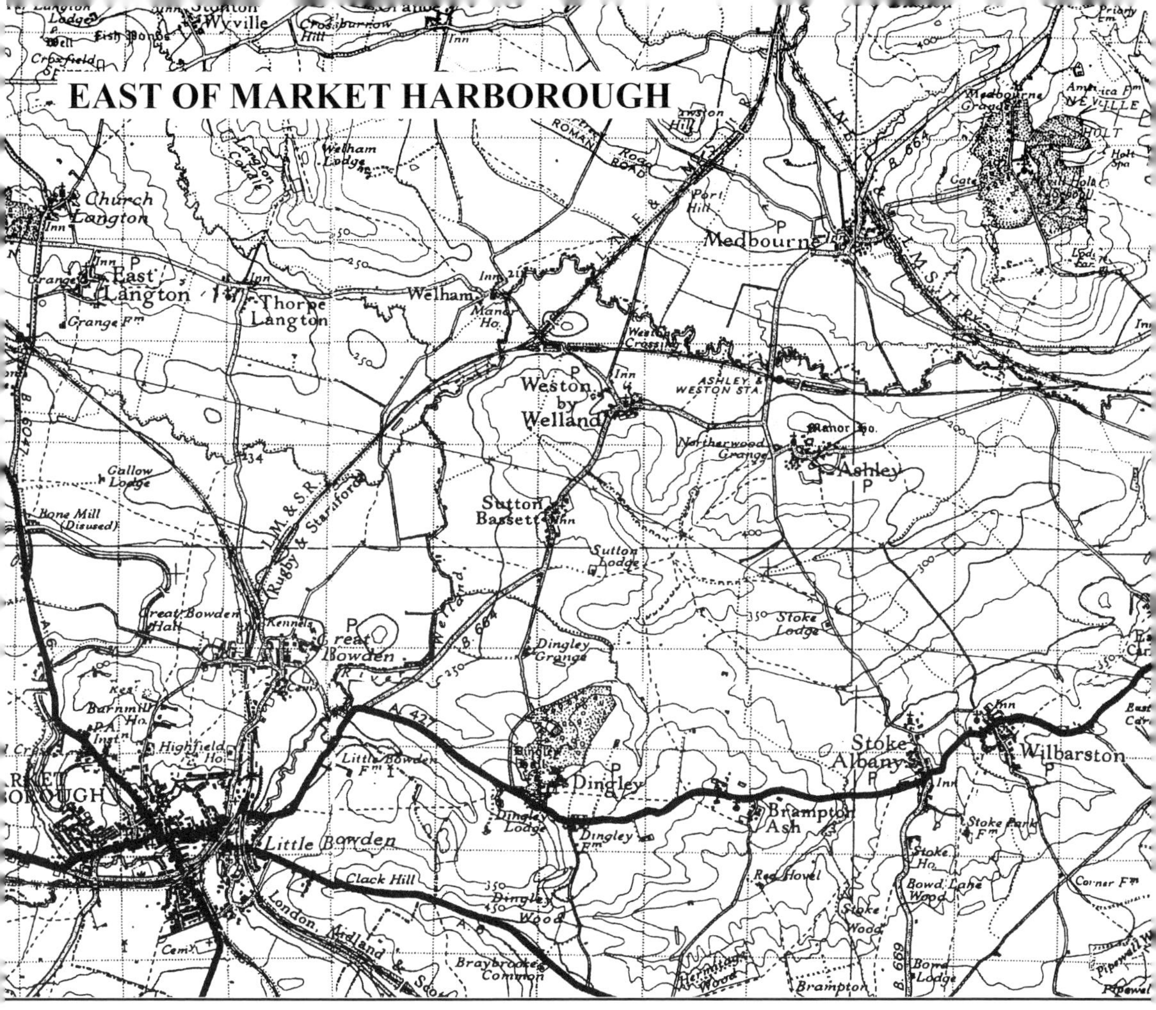

III. The 1946 edition is scaled at almost 1in to 1 mile and has the line to Rugby above the lower left corner. Higher on the left border is the route to Leicester and at the lower border is the Kettering track, marked London Midland & S. To the left of that is a short part of the line to Northampton. The Leicester-Kettering route continues in use. At the top is the line to Melton Mowbray, disused after 1963. South of Welham are extensive sidings. Their signal box closed on 13th November 1949.

PETERBRO', MARKET HARBRO', and RUGBY.—L. & N. W.

Thorpe Station,	mrn	mrn	mrn	b	aft	
NORWICH 105 dep	....	7 30	8 30	1115	2 5	....
Down.	mrn	mrn	aft	aft	aft	
Peterbro' ....dep	8 45	1030	1225	2 10	6 5	....
Wansford	8 57	1040	1235	2 22	6 17	....
Nassington..........	9 3	....	....	2 28	6 23	....
King's Cliffe ....[den	9 12	1050	....	2 37	6 32	....
Wakerley & Barrow-	9 22	....	....	2 47	6 42	....
Seaton	9 32	11 5	1257	2 57	6 52	....
Rockingham	9 41	....	....	3 7	7 2	....
Ashley and Weston..	9 51	....	....	3 18	7 13	....
Market Harbro' ar	10 2	1128	1 19	3 31	7 25	....
Market Harbro' dp	10 7	1131	1 21	3 35	7 26	....
Lubenham	1012	....	....	3 41	7 31	....
Theddingworth......	....	....	....	3 48	a	....
Welford & Kilworth.	1027	1148	....	3 57	7 42	....
Yelvertoft	....	....	....	4 5	7 50	....
Lilbourne	....	a	....	4 10	7 56	....
Clifton Mill	....	....	....	4 18	....	....
Rugby 140, 156..arr	1040	12 5	1 50	4 25	8 5	....
141 BIRMINGHAM * arr	1215	1 20	3 20	6 0	9 15	....
141 LIVERPOOL † .. „	2 40	3 15	5 5	7 45	3 0	....
190 MANCHESTER ‡ „	2 40	4 0	5 0	7 30	2 45	....

London Road Sta.,	mrn	b	mrn	aft	aft
190 MANCHESTER dep	....	7 45	9 30	1 15	4 15
144 LIVERPOOL † .. „	3c45	7 20	9 15	12 0	4 0
145 BIRMINGHAM * „	7 35	9 30	1110	4 0	6 0
Up.	mrn	mrn	aft	exp	aft
Rugby ....dep	8 30	1050	1220	4 55	7 10
Clifton Mill	8 34	....	a	....	a
Lilbourne	8 40	....	1230	....	7 20
Yelvertoft	8 46	....	1236	....	7 26
Welford & Kilworth.	8 55	11 5	1245	....	7 35
Theddingworth......	9 3	....	a	....	7 43
Lubenham	9 9	....	1257	....	7 49
Market Harbro' ar	9 15	1122	1 3	5 21	7 55
Market Harbro' dp	9 17	1124	1 5	5 22	7 57
Ashley and Weston..	9 28	1135	1 16	d	8 8
Rockingham	9 40	1146	1 28	d	8 20
Seaton ....[den	9 49	1156	1 37	5 53	8 29
Wakerley & Barrow-	9 59	....	1 49	a	8 39
King's Cliffe	10 9	1210	1 59	6 10	8 49
Nassington..........	1018	....	2 8	....	8 58
Wansford 121	1024	1220	2 14	6 22	9 4
Peterbro' 107, 106 arr	1040	1230	2 30	6 35	9 20
NORWICH 104 arr	....	3 50	6 40	....	2 0

a Stop by signal to take up, and set down on informing the Guard at the preceding *stopping* Station. **b** Through carriage between Norwich and Birmingham and Wolverhampton. *c* Leaves at 3 mrn. on Mondays. **d** Stops by signal to take up for Peterbro' and beyond. * New Street. † Lime Street. ‡ London Road.

April 1880

ASHLEY & WESTON

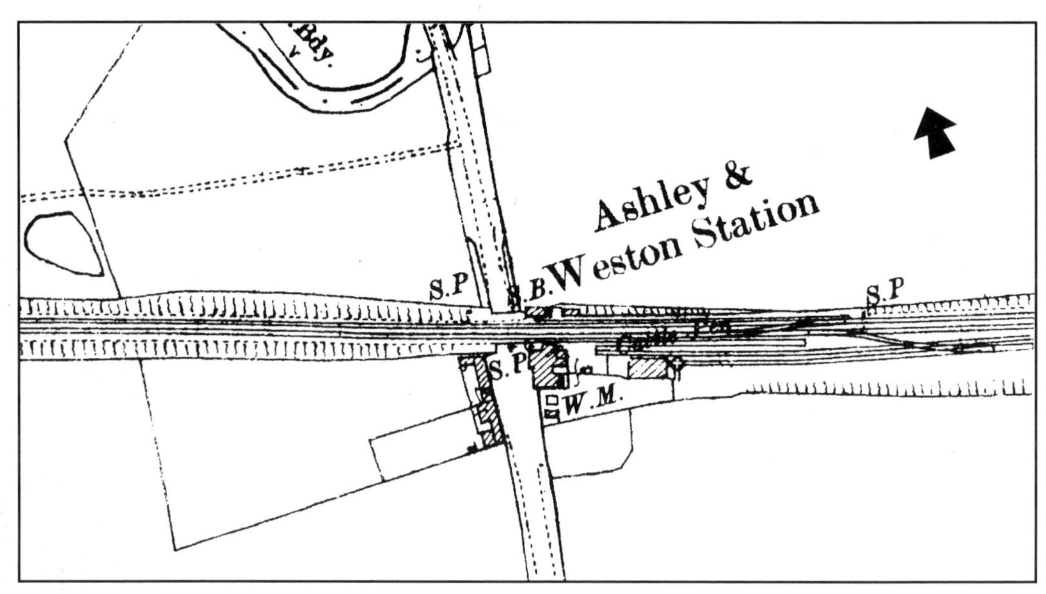

IV. The goods shed is to the right of the weighing machine, on this 1900 edition. A 25cwt crane was listed in 1938.

5. This station is right of centre on map III and south of it is Ashley, which had 192 residents in 1901. This postcard view is westwards and is from about the 1950s. Opened on 1st June 1850 as 'Medbourne Bridge', it received the name shown on 1st January 1880.
(D.Rokeby/R.Humm)

6. Closure to passengers came on 18th June 1951, but railway staff could still use it on Fridays, for a year. Prior to that date, there were three down and two up trains calling on weekdays. The goods yard closed on 18th March 1963. The box opened in September 1879 and its 24-lever frame was taken out of use on 28th January 1968. There had been another box at Holts Siding from 1873 to about 1899 and also at Drayton Junction from 1879 to 2nd January 1945. (Milepost 92½)

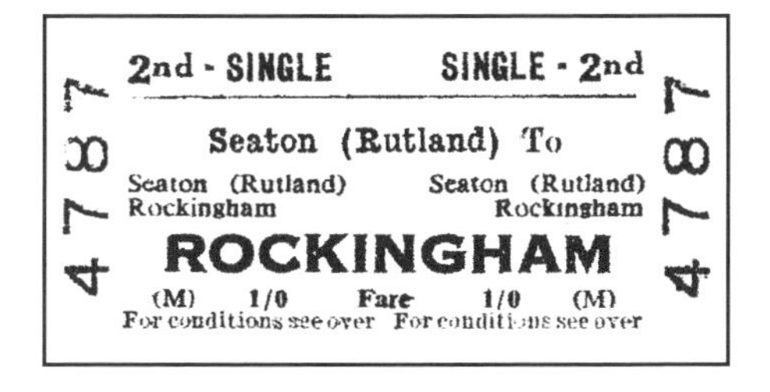

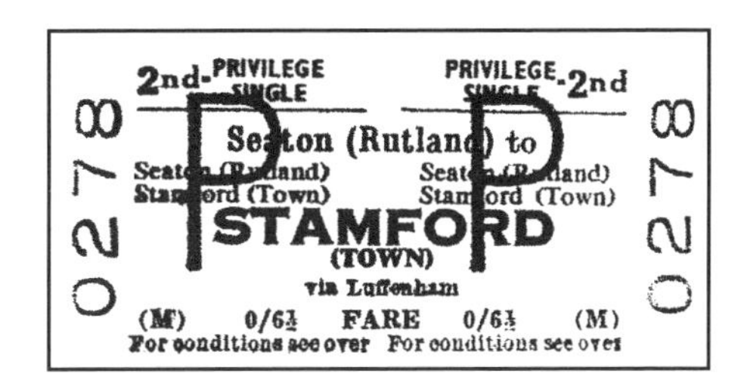

ROCKINGHAM

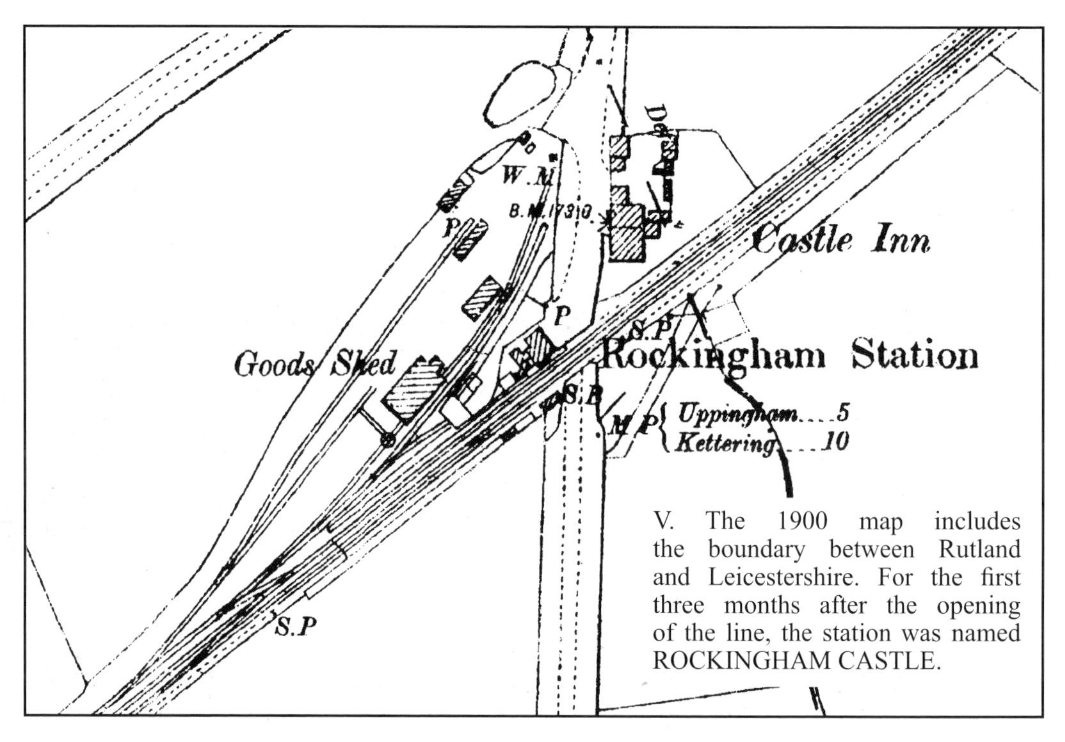

V. The 1900 map includes the boundary between Rutland and Leicestershire. For the first three months after the opening of the line, the station was named ROCKINGHAM CASTLE.

7. Track doubling took place in 1873 in this district. This postcard view is after that, but before road surfacing. The Castle Hotel is on the left. (P.Laming coll.)

8. Waiting with freight on 22nd April 1959 is class 4F 0-6-0 no. 44097, which was ex-LMS. The village had a population of 135 in 1961. The fine building remains standing, in use as a dwelling. (H.C.Casserley)

9. A broader view on the same day includes part of the goods yard, which was in use until 6th April 1964. Passenger service lasted here until 6th June 1966. The 1879 signal box had 24 levers and was worked until 28th January 1968. (H.C.Casserley)

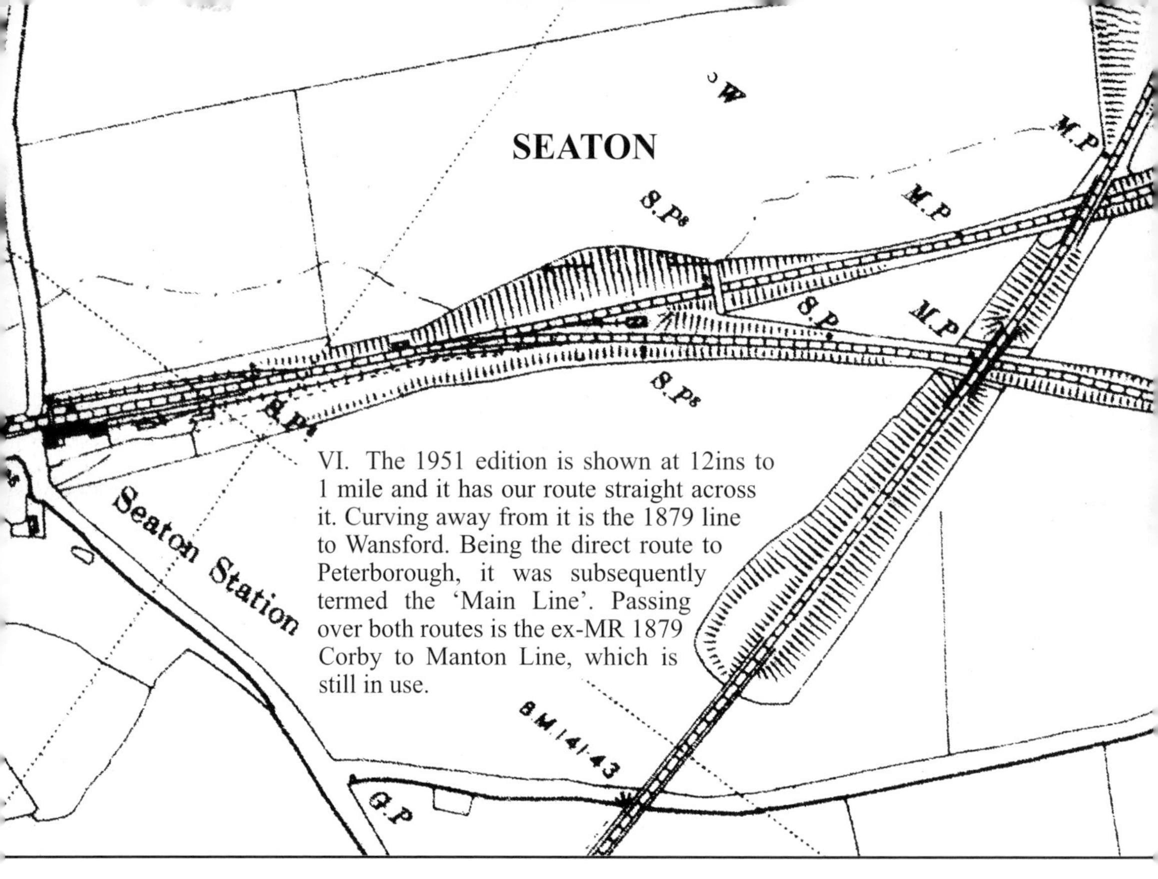

VI. The 1951 edition is shown at 12ins to 1 mile and it has our route straight across it. Curving away from it is the 1879 line to Wansford. Being the direct route to Peterborough, it was subsequently termed the 'Main Line'. Passing over both routes is the ex-MR 1879 Corby to Manton Line, which is still in use.

10. We are looking down at the branch platform on 1st May 1954, with ex-GNR class C12 4-4-2T no. 67368 on the 2.57pm to Stamford (Town) and, at the outer end, ex-LNWR 2-4-2T no. 46604, with the 2.54pm to Uppingham. A Rugby to Peterborough train is signalled at the down main platform. The 48-lever box is below this signal and it was in use from 1879 until 6th June 1966. There were occasional freight movements subsequently, mainly for minerals, for two years. (N.W.Sprinks)

11. In the down bay on 21st April 1958 is ex-LMS class 3F 0-6-0T no. 47300 with the 11.10am to Uppingham. The crossover had earlier been controlled from a ground frame at the far end of the left platform. Seaton had 240 residents in 1901 and there were then five other places of the same name, some near the sea. (R.M.Casserley)

For other views, see pictures 88 to 96 in *Northampton to Peterborough* **in the 'Country Railway Routes' series from Middleton Press. This includes the reopened Nene Valley Railway.**

12. The tiny engine shed is seen on the same day and is shown on the map. No. 41214 is a class 2MT 2-6-2T, a type introduced by the LMS in 1946. Local goods traffic here ceased on 6th April 1964. The route to Luffenham Junction was singled on 21st July 1907. (R.M.Casserley)

UPPINGHAM

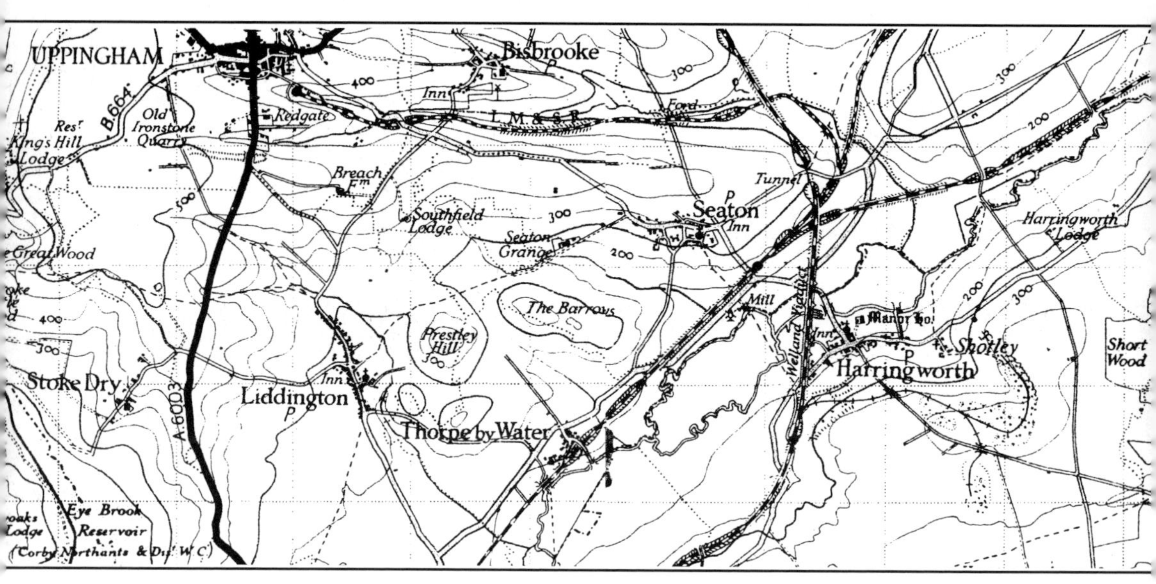

VII. The entire branch is shown on the 1946 edition at 1in to 1 mile. See caption VI for the destinations of the other lines. Seaton station is southeast of the village of that name.

13. A fine early postcard shows the climb to the town centre. The spire is close to the famous school (founded in 1584), which was able to run three special trains on 27th September 1894, four days before the branch opened to the public. (P.Laming coll.)

14. It is 1st May 1954 and the class C12 4-4-2T no. 67368 is about to depart at 1.55pm and run the 3½ mile length of the branch, with its ex-LMS coach. It was ex-GNR. Many cattle pens are evident, as are the ground frame levers. There was never a signal box here. (N.W.Sprinks)

VIII. The 1951 extract is at 12ins to 1 mile and features the well-known public school, Uppingham School, which generated much traffic. The population was 2588 in 1901 and 1940 in 1961.

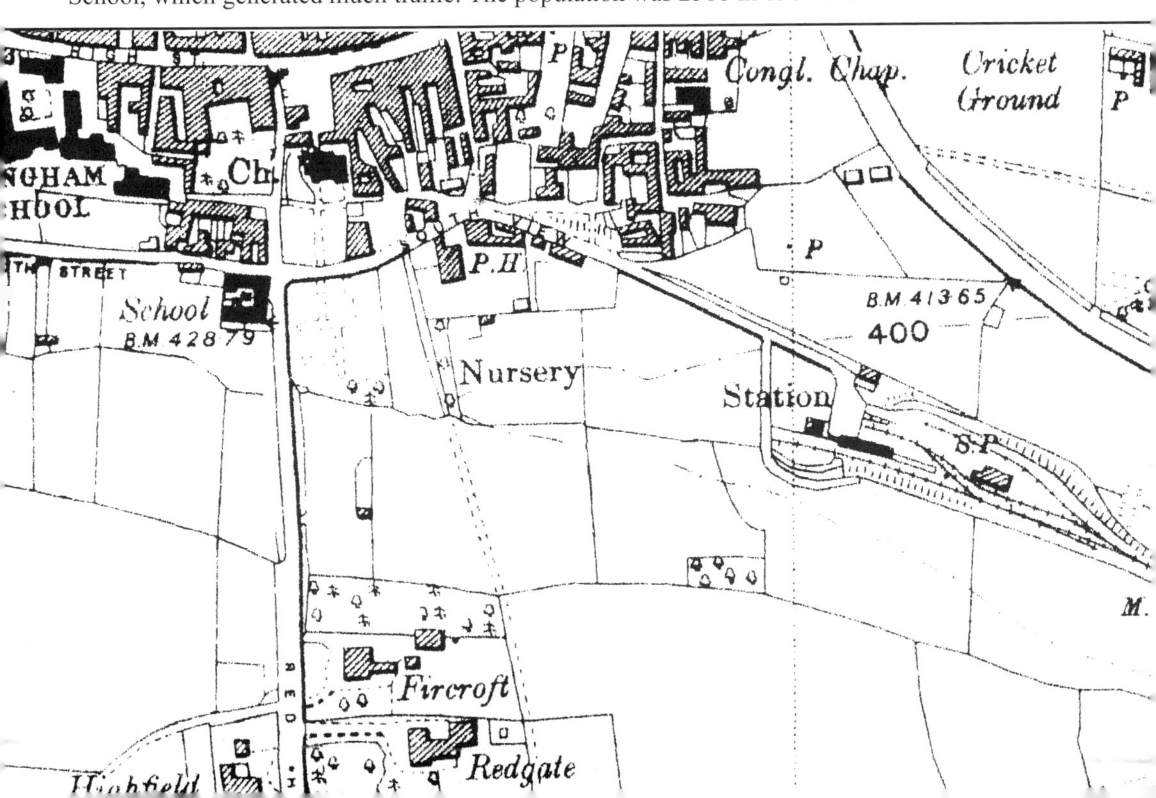

15. Almost at the end of the line on 26th July 1958 is class 2MT 2-6-2T no. 41214. The elegant 'Schools' class 4-4-0 express locomotives of the Southern Railway were all named after the best schools. However, this local school objected and no. 923 had to be renamed *Bradfield* in 1933. It was the only one to object in this way. (R.J.Buckley/Initial Photographics)

16. The 5-ton crane is not visible in this panorama from 23rd April 1959. In the distance is no. 41975, a class 3P 4-4-2T. Passenger service ceased on 13th June 1960, but school specials were allowed until 30th May 1964. Freight ceased two days later. (H.C.Casserley)

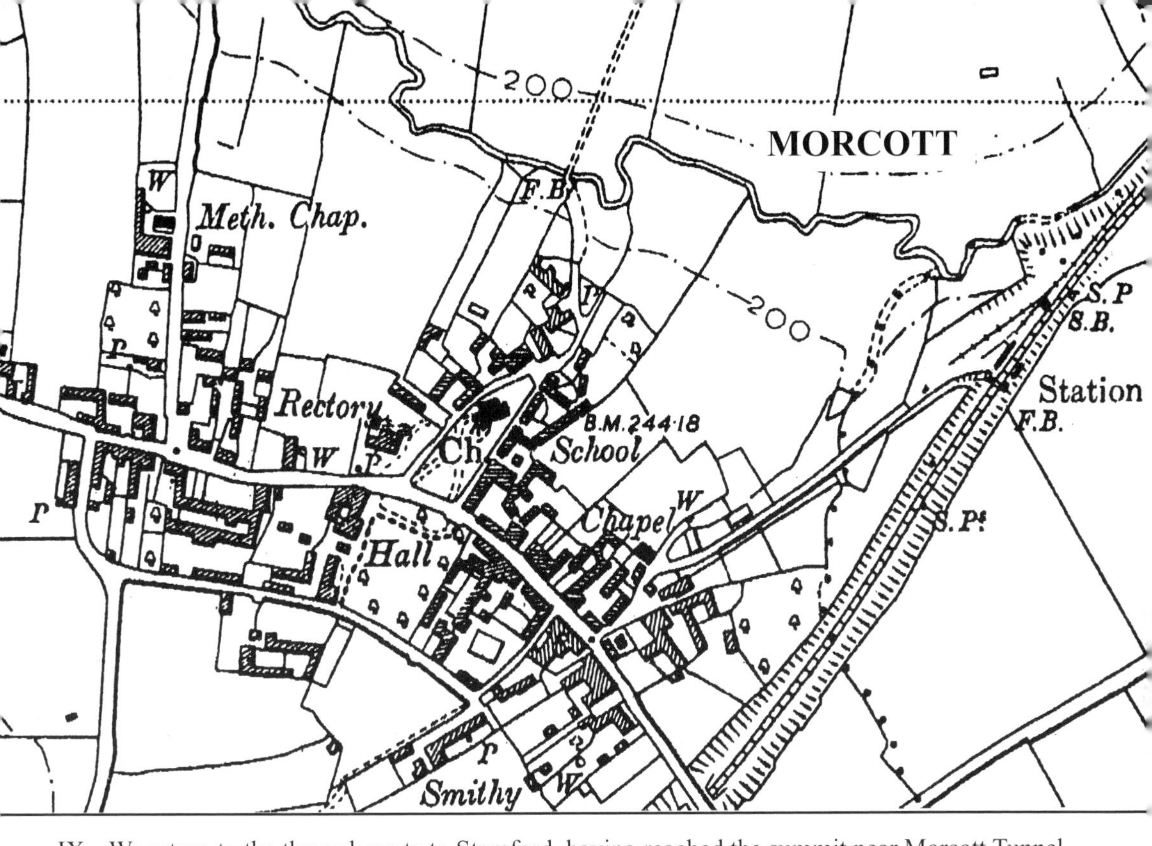

IX. We return to the through route to Stamford, having reached the summit near Morcott Tunnel. The 1901 edition is at 12ins to 1 mile and includes a small northern tributary of the River Chater.

17. We look up the approach road on 23rd April 1959 and see the prospective passenger's perspective and the photographer's 1934 Hillman Minx. The goods yard closed on 4th May 1964. (H.C.Casserley)

18. The station received passengers from 31st October 1898 to 6th June 1966. There had been a second platform in use on the right, together with a signal box, until July 1907. (R.M.Casserley)

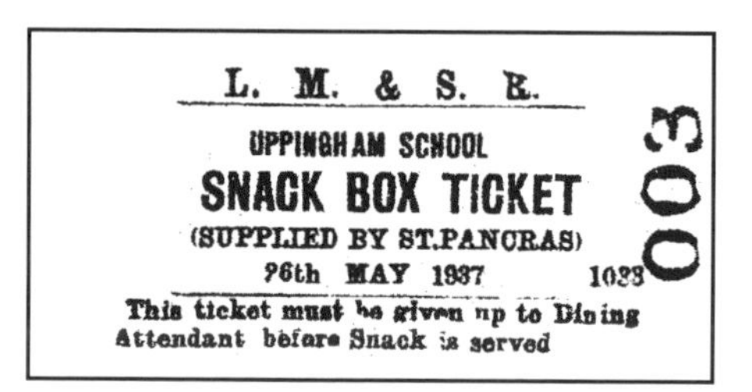

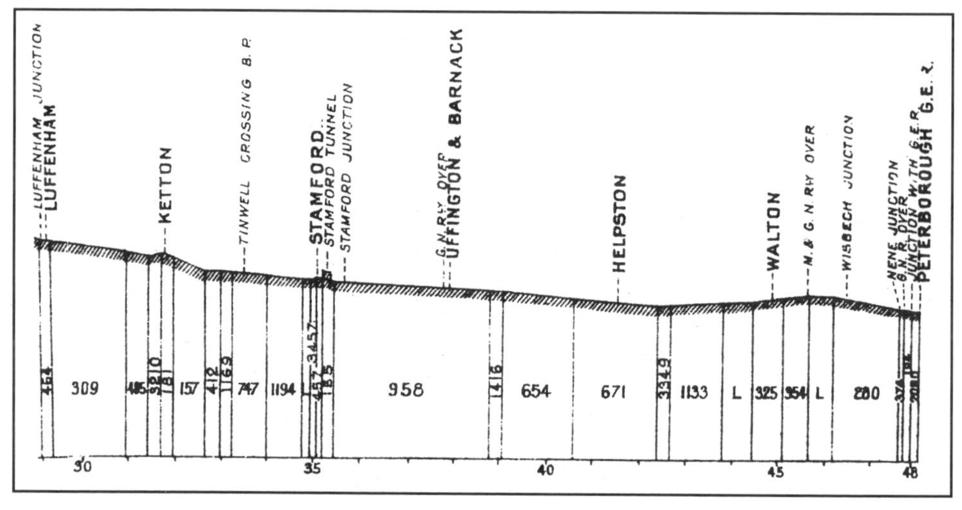

X. The MR part of the route is included here. We cannot trace gradient profiles for most other lines herein.

LUFFENHAM

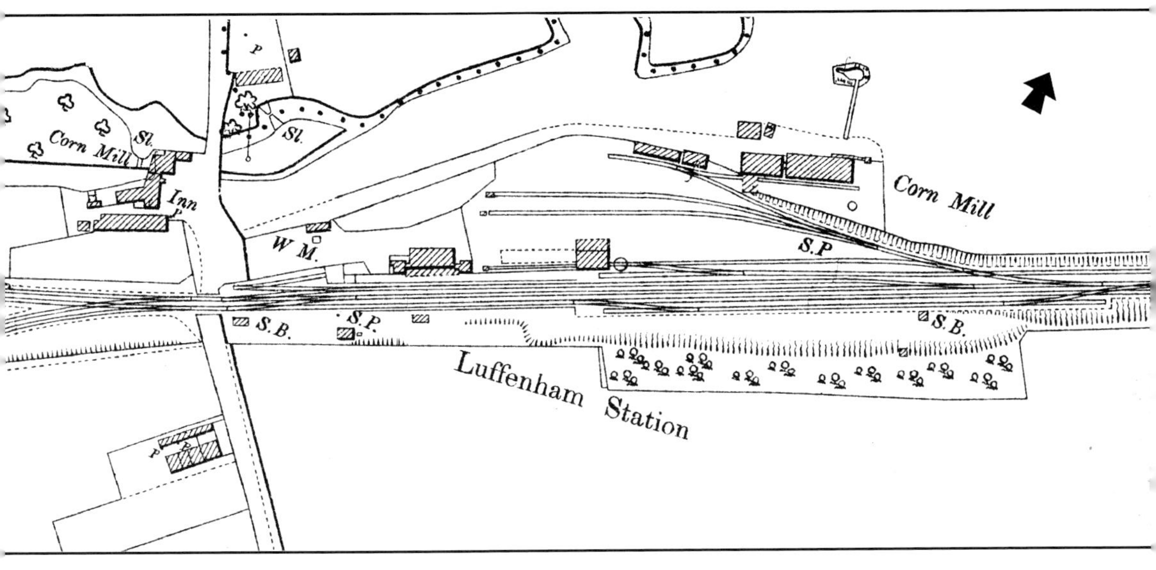

XI. The LNWR route from Seaton is the lower one on the left and the MR is across the page on this 1904 extract at 20ins to 1 mile. The River Chater meanders at the top.

19. The junction signals are evident in this postcard view westwards in about 1900. The station received passengers from 1st May 1848 until 6th June 1966. (LOSA)

20. In the distance is a van in the goods yard, which closed on 4th May 1964. On opposite sides of the line were North Luffenham and South Luffenham. In 1901, they housed 443 and 290 souls, respectively. (P.Laming coll.)

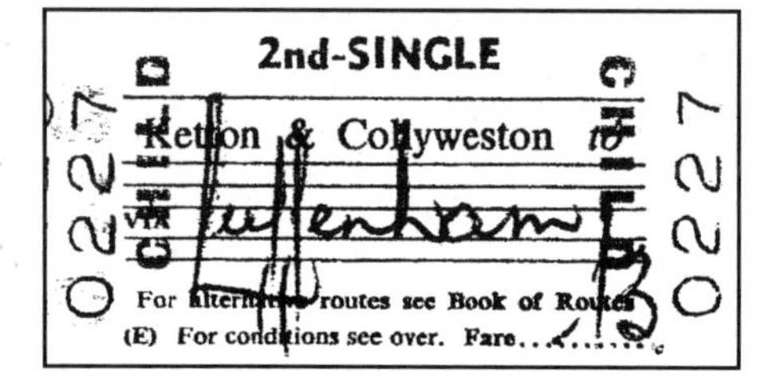

21. Luffenham Junction Box had 35 levers and it lasted until 11th March 1990. It is just beyond the train, which is being propelled by an unidentifiable locomotive, towards Seaton. Oakham-Peterborough trains continue to run through the site. (SLS coll.)

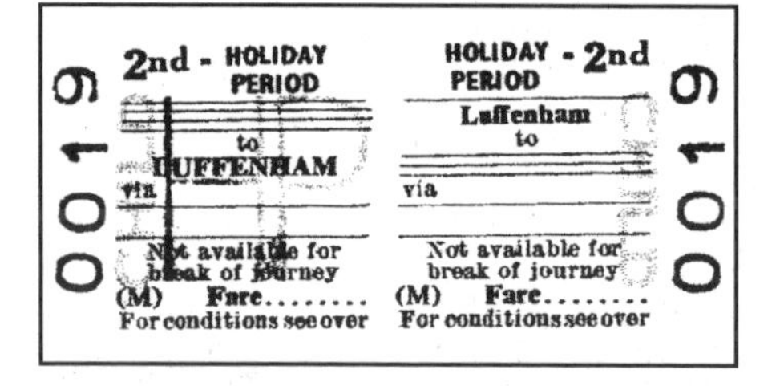

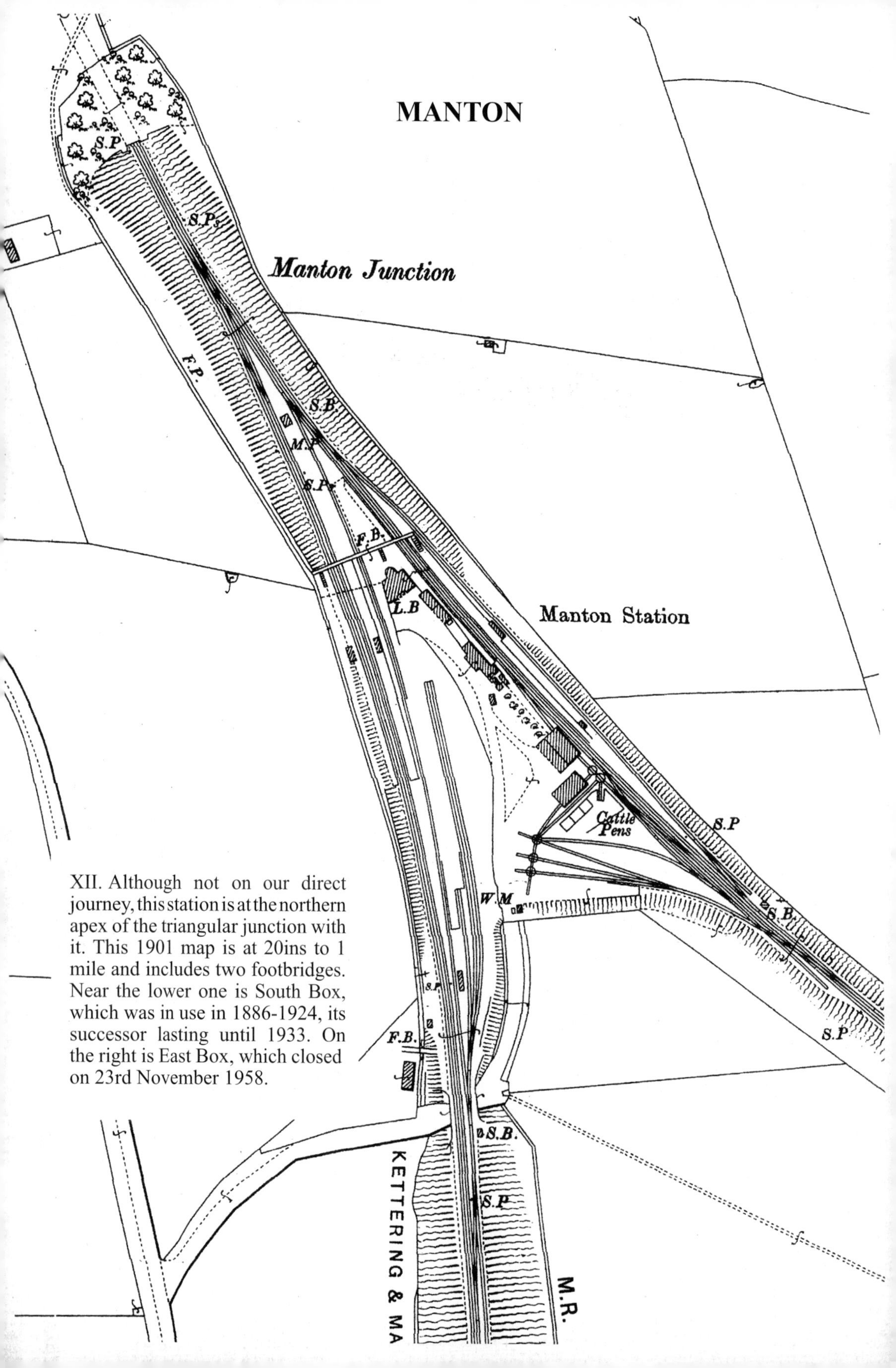

XII. Although not on our direct journey, this station is at the northern apex of the triangular junction with it. This 1901 map is at 20ins to 1 mile and includes two footbridges. Near the lower one is South Box, which was in use in 1886-1924, its successor lasting until 1933. On the right is East Box, which closed on 23rd November 1958.

22. The entrance is seen from the goods yard in about 1963. Having passed through the booking hall, passengers had to use the footbridge to reach any one of the four platforms. (Milepost 92½)

23. This view north is from the same day and includes the southern portal of Manton Tunnel, which is 749yds long. The village is on top of it. The name of the station was 'Manton for Uppingham' until 1st October 1934. (Milepost 92½)

24. All four signs were as helpful as the one on the left in this photo from 31st May 1963. The 'Robin Hood' express between St. Pancras and Nottingham called here from 1959 to 1962, but was otherwise non-stop between the latter and Kettering. (H.C.Casserley)

25. No. 31412 comes off the Stamford line at Manton Junction with the 15.52 Cambridge-Birmingham New Street train on 3rd July 1983. The short wooden signal post next to the train is an unusual feature. The track curving round behind the box formed part of an up loop on the Corby line. The station had closed to goods on 4th May 1964 and passengers on 6th June 1966. (P.D.Shannon)

Pictures 35 to 44 in the *Kettering to Nottingham* album give other views of this location.

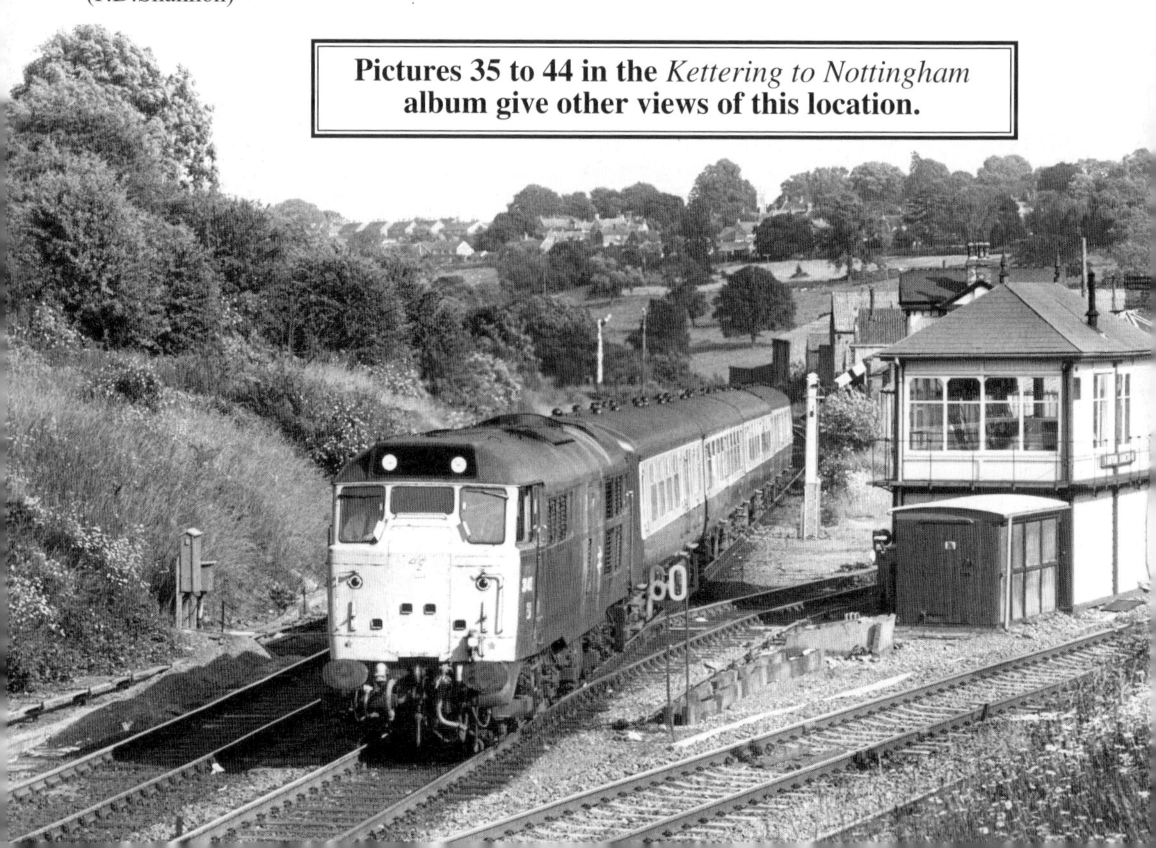

26. A panorama from above the tunnel mouth on 15th March 2014 includes the 1913 Junction Box. Its 35-lever frame was replaced by a panel on 24th July 1988. The main buildings can still be seen. No. 170112 is bound for Birmingham New Street. (J.Whitehouse)

KETTON & COLLYWESTON

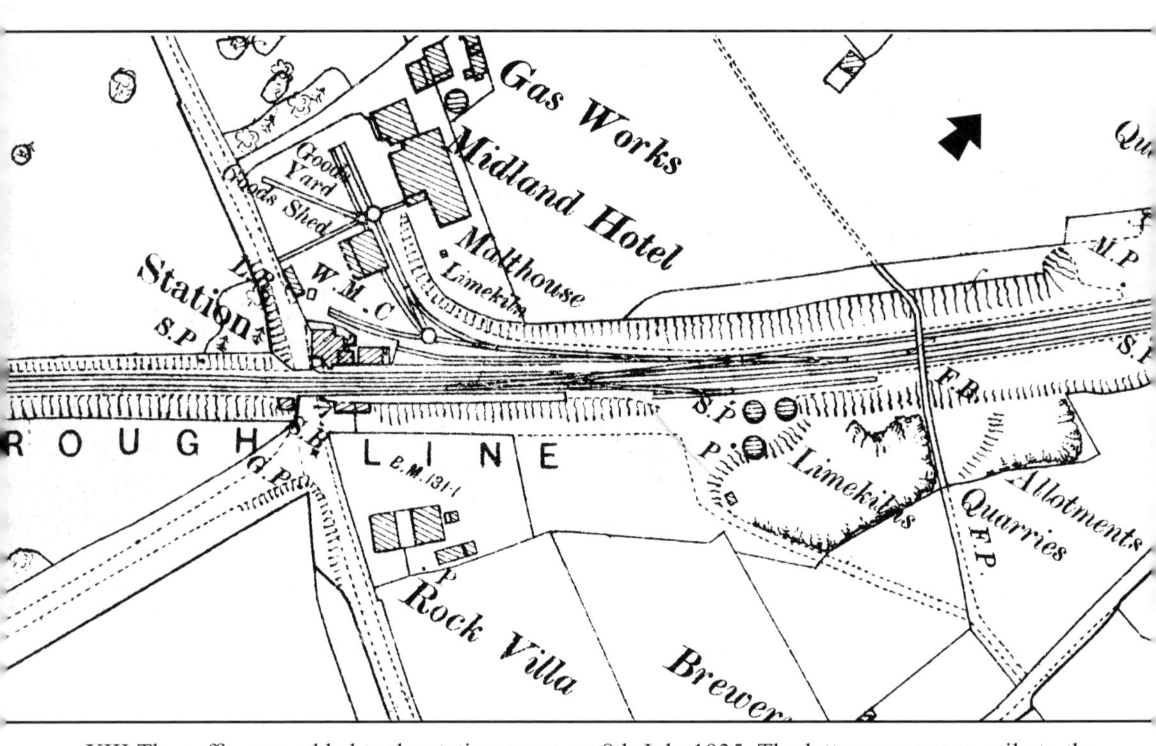

XIII. The suffix was added to the station name on 8th July 1935. The latter was over a mile to the south. The 1901 survey is at 20ins to 1 mile. The goods yard had a 10-ton crane. Ketton housed 1041 in 1901 and 1142 in 1961.

27. On the left is the 20-lever signal box, with wicket gates close to it. Its frame and semaphore signals were still in use in 2016, but all the gates had been replaced by full barriers, controlled from the box. (P.Laming coll.)

28. The 3.4pm departure was recorded on 7th October 1950, hauled by ex-LNER class C12 4-4-2T no. 67362. It had been built by the GNR. Four private sidings were listed nearby in 1938: ICI (Lime) Ltd, Ketton Architectural Stone Co. Ltd, Ketton Portland Cement Co. Ltd and Woolston & Bull's Siding. (P.Wells/SLS)

29. From a passing train in 1953 we can enjoy the flowers in full bloom and the discreet entrance for gentlemen in need. The platform lamps are lit by oil, although the gas works was adjacent. (R.M.Casserley)

30. We can now enjoy two photos from 21st April 1958. Platform access was via the small gates. The goods yard closed on 26th April 1965 and passenger service ceased on 6th June 1966. Signs had improved. (R.M.Casserley)

31. Known as a Victorian Ecclesiastical Tudor pattern, the station was built of local stone, with Collyweston stone slate roofing. There is no evidence of the belfry ever having had a bell. Local judgement resulted in demolition of everything. (R.M.Casserley)

WEST OF STAMFORD

32. The cement works is at the eastern border of Ketton and shunting was recorded on 28th January 2016. This location is north of the exchange sidings and class 08s are at work. There have been regular open days, sometimes with steam. It was in Hanson ownership and a bat cave has been created. (A.C.Mott)

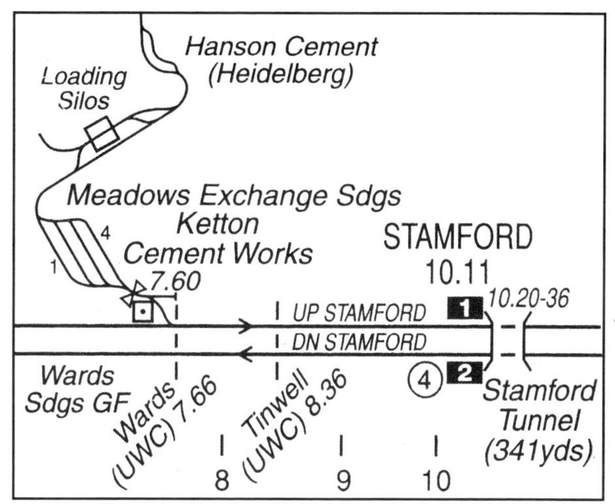

XIV. Wards Siding Ground Frame came into use in 1928 and it was a signal box from 1930 to 1963. This diagram is from 2013. (© TRACKmaps)

33. This cement train from Ketton Works was photographed from the A1 overbridge on 13th April 1984. No. 25194 is providing the power and the chimneys are in the background. The train is bound for West Bromwich, but the loco will have to run round the train at Peterborough and return on the adjacent track. (P.D.Shannon)

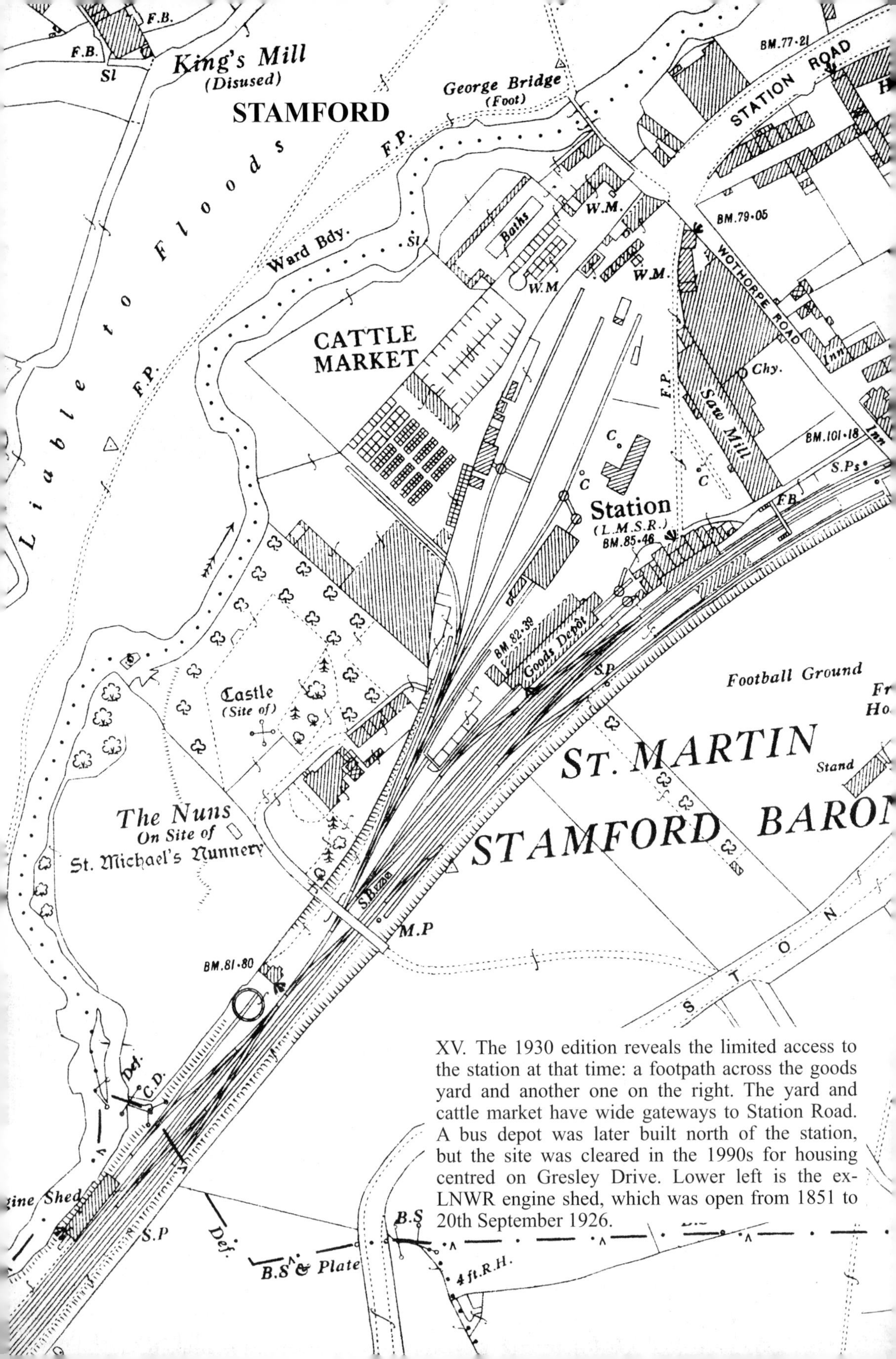

XV. The 1930 edition reveals the limited access to the station at that time: a footpath across the goods yard and another one on the right. The yard and cattle market have wide gateways to Station Road. A bus depot was later built north of the station, but the site was cleared in the 1990s for housing centred on Gresley Drive. Lower left is the ex-LNWR engine shed, which was open from 1851 to 20th September 1926.

34. The second path just mentioned is evident opposite the Telegraph Inn. The telegraph used codes along wires, before telephones came into use. This is an MR official view, dated 1889, when inside track keys were still used. The first station was beyond the bridges and tunnel from 2nd October 1846 until 19th June 1848. A shovel was essential in stations with the introduction of corridor trains. (R.S.Carpenter coll.)

35. The running-in board has no suffix. TOWN was added from 25th September 1950 until 18th April 1966. The main item of importance is the barrow crossing. Note also the ash excreted by waiting locomotives; another reason for shovels to be handy, for use before the crossing catches fire. (P.Laming coll.)

36. It is 28th August 1947 and LMS class 1P 0-4-4T no. 1416 waits in the bay with the 8.50am to Seaton. The canopy tracery is worthy of study, as are the joys of a ZUBE. TOWN was added to the name in 1950. (W.A.Camwell/SLS)

37. This train is arriving from Seaton in about 1952. It is being hauled by an ex-LNWR 2-4-2T. The driver will be at the right window on the return journey and the white lamp will be replaced by a red painted one. (W.A.Camwell/SLS)

38. No. 40452 is an ex-MR class 2P 4-4-0 of a batch of over 140 built in 1891-1901. The view is from the early 1950s and includes the station's coal supply and its weather vane, which includes the letters S & PR. The suffix TOWN was dropped on 18th April 1966. (W.A.Camwell/SLS)

39. The vane is seen again, together with the fine north elevation. It was listed Grade II. Goods traffic ceased here on 22nd November 1967 and car parking areas were steadily extended. This is the scene on 4th December 1980. (D.A.Thompson)

40. Overnight snow lingers on the track and platforms as a Cravens two-car unit formed of cars E51298 and E56443, calls with a morning train from Peterborough on 8th January 1982. At that time Cravens units were common across East Anglia and Lincolnshire. Just beyond the station building is the goods yard, which remained in use as a coal yard until 16th May 1983. Stamford signal box closed on 15th May 1984 and its functions were transferred to Ketton. It had opened on 16th March 1895. (P.D.Shannon)

41. The intricate rooflines of railway and non-railway buildings merge to create an interesting backdrop for no. 31421, as it pulls away with the 09.35 Norwich-Birmingham New Street train on 13th April 1984. The combination of a Mark 1 BG (gangwayed brake van) and early Mark 2 passenger stock was common on cross-country services at that time, the Mark 2 vehicles providing a rather more comfortable ride than the DMUs they had recently replaced. (P.D.Shannon)

42. To add to the variety of stock to have used the route, we witness no. 158850 on 4th April 1998 working the 14.05 Cambridge to Birmingham New Street. By that time, the ticket office was open weekday mornings only. Stamford East and the junction are shown later, in pictures 85 to 95. (B.I.Nathan)

43. The map shows the position of the signal box, just north of the turntable. The retired box was moved to the position shown on 13th December 1988, to serve as a store for the railway bookshop, which had been created by Robert Humm in the main building. He rented it from 1986 to 2016, when the business was moved into the town. No. 66130 is seen with freight on 4th May 2011. Passenger usage was nearing 0.3m annually by this time. (J.Whitehouse)

UFFINGTON & BARNACK

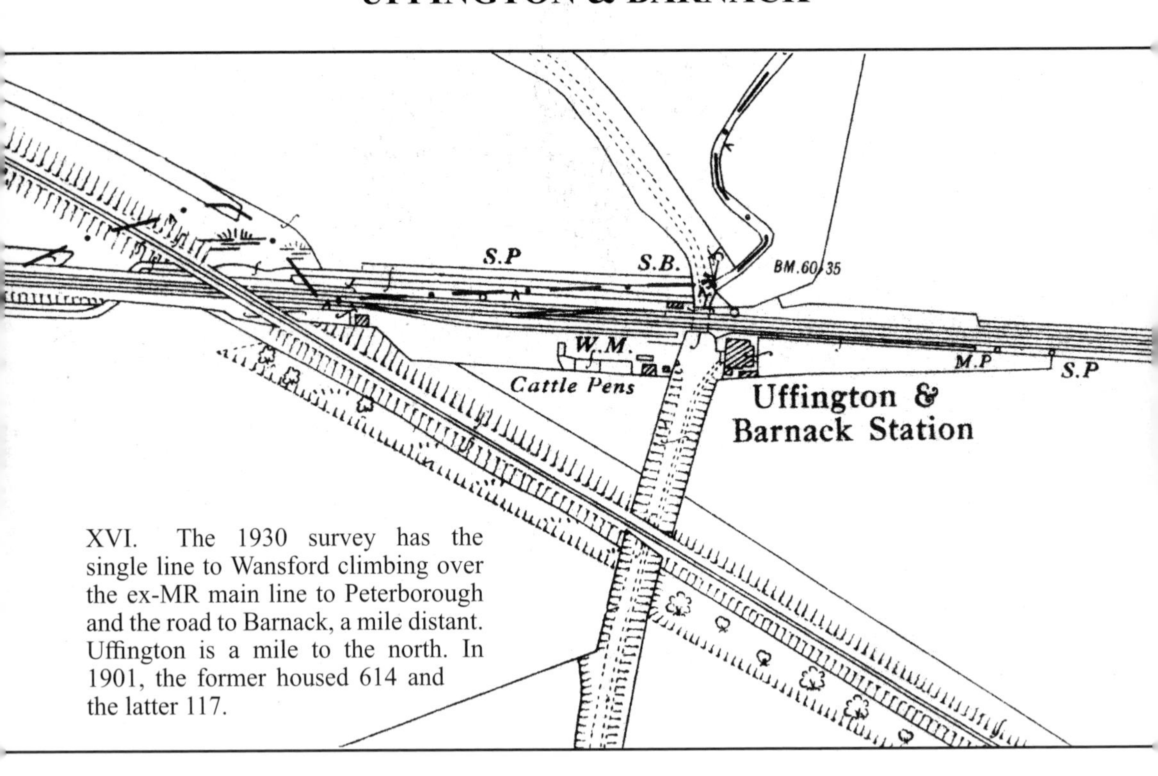

XVI. The 1930 survey has the single line to Wansford climbing over the ex-MR main line to Peterborough and the road to Barnack, a mile distant. Uffington is a mile to the north. In 1901, the former housed 614 and the latter 117.

44. This undated view under the bridge does not show that the left span is over a stream. The Wansford branch was leased by the GNR from 18th December 1893. It had been opened on 6th August 1867 by the S&ER. (R.M.Casserley coll.)

45. It is 6th September 1957 and ex-WD 2-8-0 no. 90340 runs west with mixed freight. The passenger platforms had been closed on 1st September 1952. 'Barnack' had been added to the name on 1st February 1858. The next station east had been Bainton Gate, but was in use in 1854-56 only. (Milepost 92½)

46. Class B1 4-6-0 no. 61205 heads the 12.52pm Leicester to Peterborough on 23rd April 1959. Near the rear coach is the connection to the goods yard, which was in use until 1st July 1963. The 16-lever box opened on 29th June 1909 and was still in use in 2016, when it still had hand-worked gates. (H.C.Casserley)

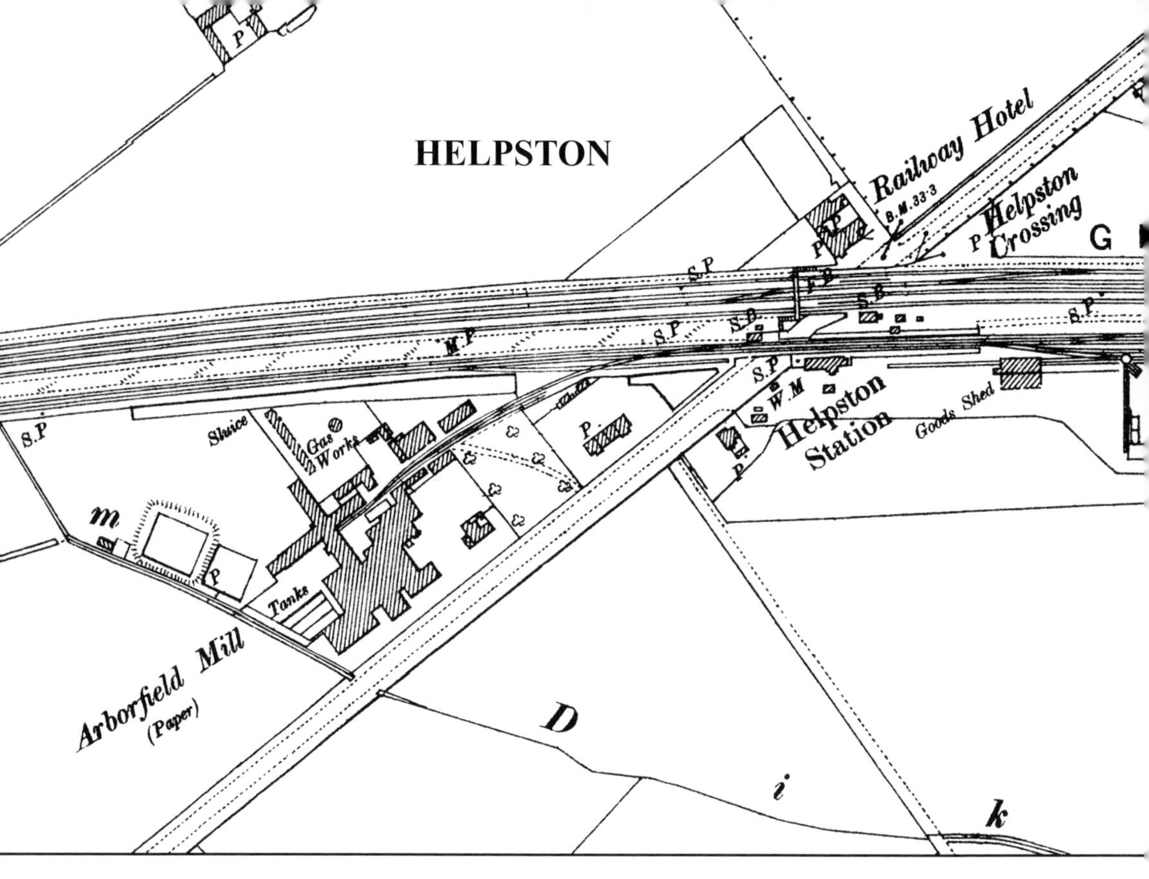

47. The station served passengers from 2nd October 1846 until 6th June 1966. There were 623 locals in 1901 and 641 in 1961. The suffix 'for Market Deeping' was used from 1858 to 1912. Goods traffic ceased on 3rd May 1965. Listed Grade II, the goods shed appears in picture 34 in our *Peterborough to Newark* album. (LOSA)

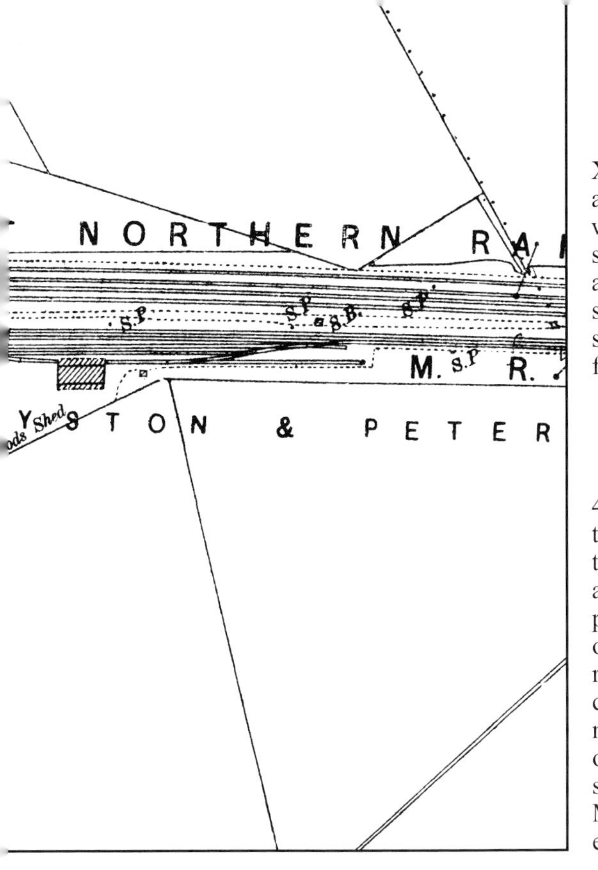

XVII. The 1852 main line of the GNR is above the 1846 MR line. The former is shown with four tracks and the latter with two, plus a station and goods yard. The map is dated 1900 and is scaled at 25ins to 1 mile. The private siding serves a paper mill. Helpston ballast sidings were about two miles westwards. The footbridge was demolished in March 1985.

48. It is 6th August 1953 and we are looking towards Peterborough with the ex-MR box on the left and the 25-lever ex-GNR one centre, along with its signals. This box received a panel on 26th July 1975. The MR box closed on 28th March 1971. Lifting barriers on both routes are still controlled from the former. It also controls four other crossings, using CCTV. The northbound line from here to a junction south of Walton was electrified on 7th March 1988. It served as the slow line for both routes, from 28th March 1971, thus only five of the six lines were electrified. (H.C.Casserley)

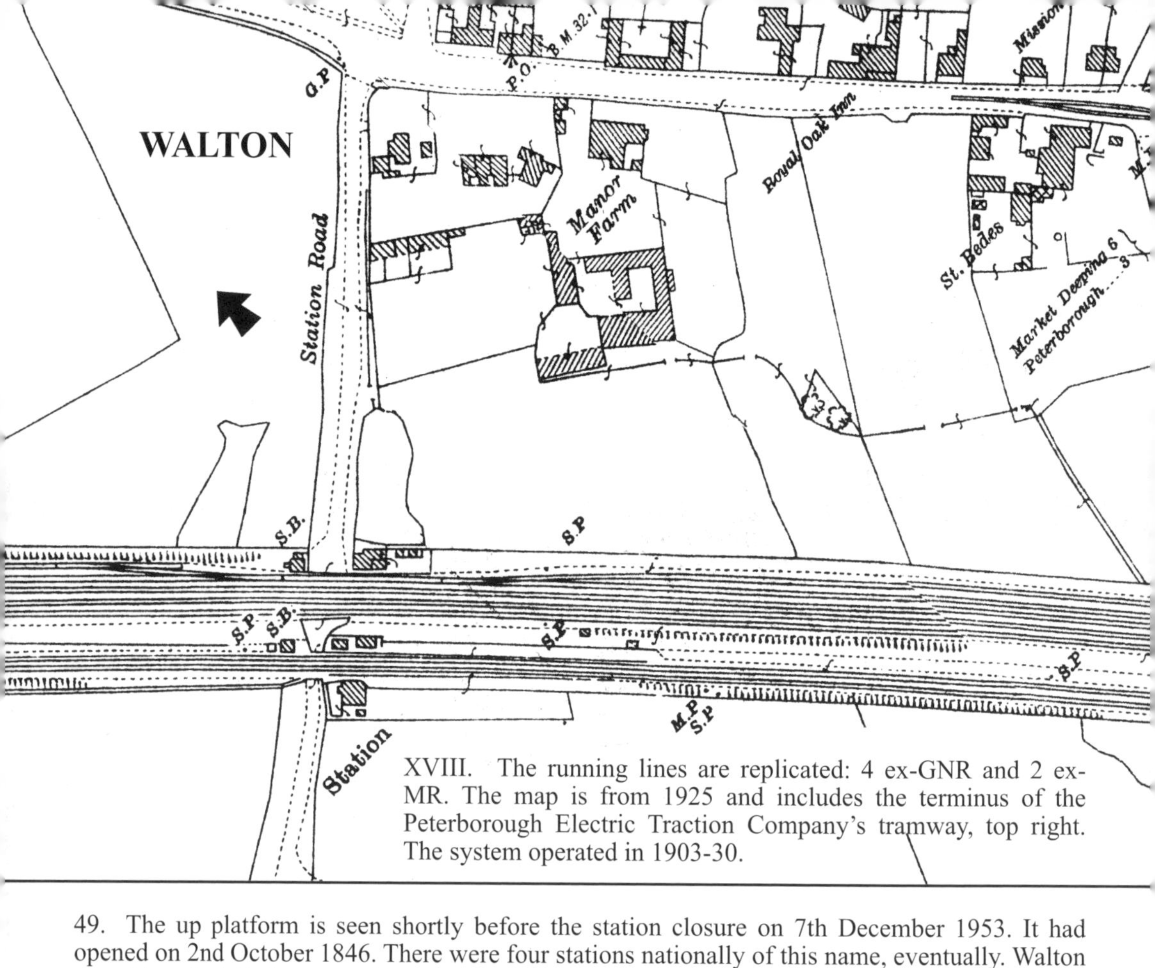

XVIII. The running lines are replicated: 4 ex-GNR and 2 ex-MR. The map is from 1925 and includes the terminus of the Peterborough Electric Traction Company's tramway, top right. The system operated in 1903-30.

49. The up platform is seen shortly before the station closure on 7th December 1953. It had opened on 2nd October 1846. There were four stations nationally of this name, eventually. Walton signal box had 12 levers and was in use from 1875 until 1971. Gate box was the term until the crossing was closed in 1976. (Milepost 92½)

50. Ex-MR class 2P 4-4-0 no. 40364 is running to Stamford around 1950, while cars wait between the crossings. Note the difference in gate lengths. The northbound ex-MR line from here to Peterborough was electrified on 16th March 1987. The GNR tracks were energised to Leeds on 24th September 1989 and used operationally from 14th May 1990. (A.Dudman coll.)

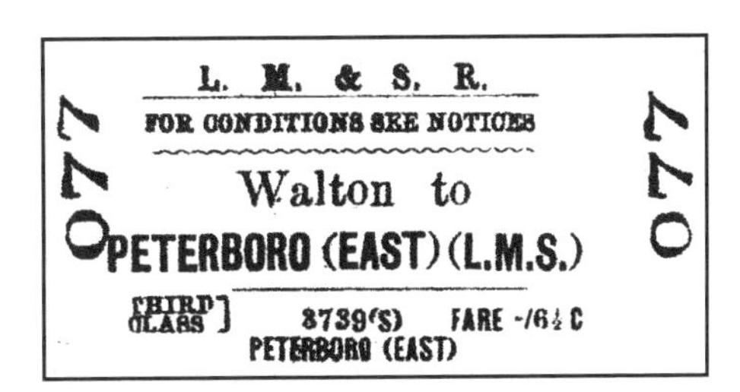

PETERBOROUGH

XIX. The MR diagram of 1916 has its lines bold. Their goods depot is lower right and their trains terminated at the adjacent GER station, termed EAST from 1923.

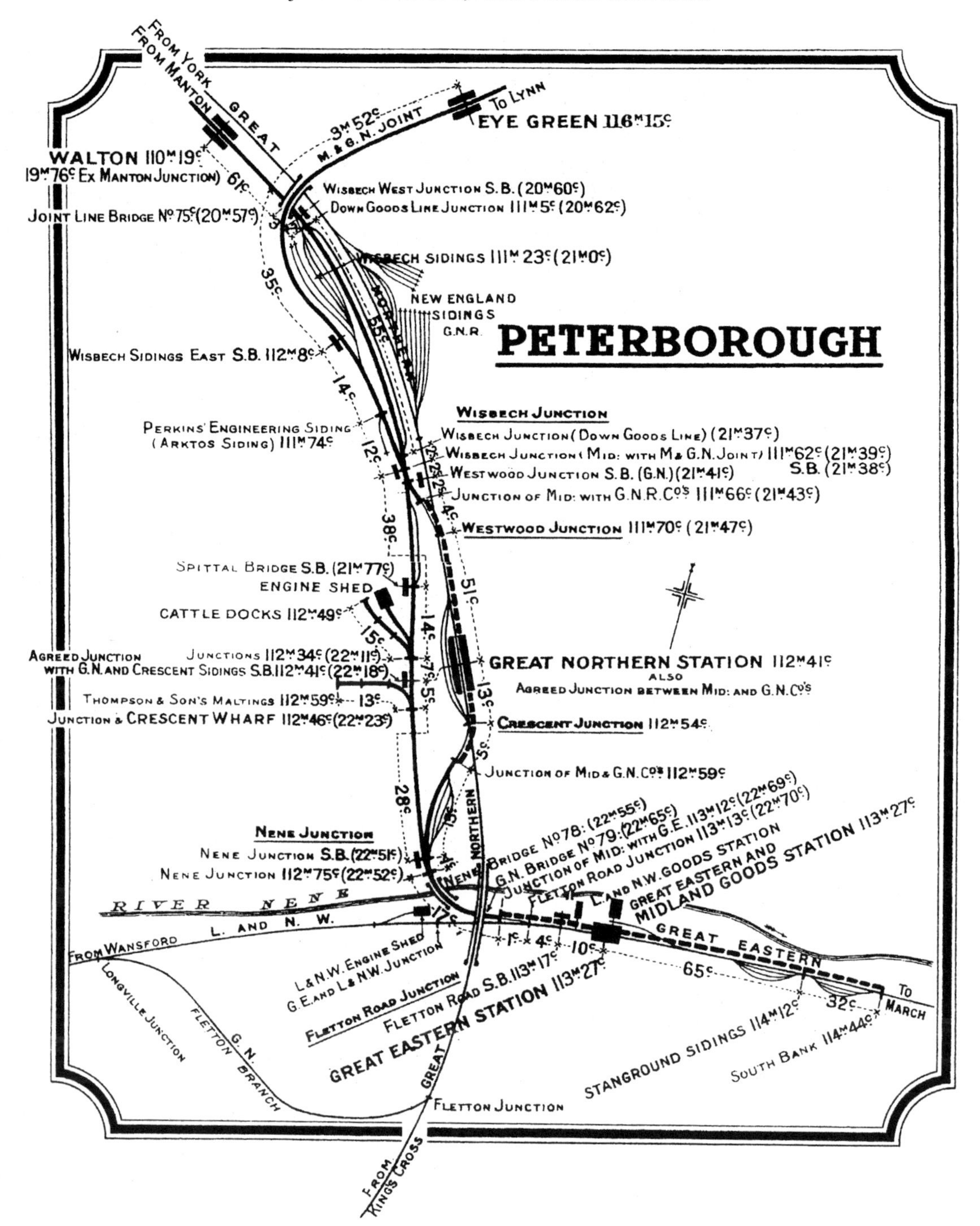

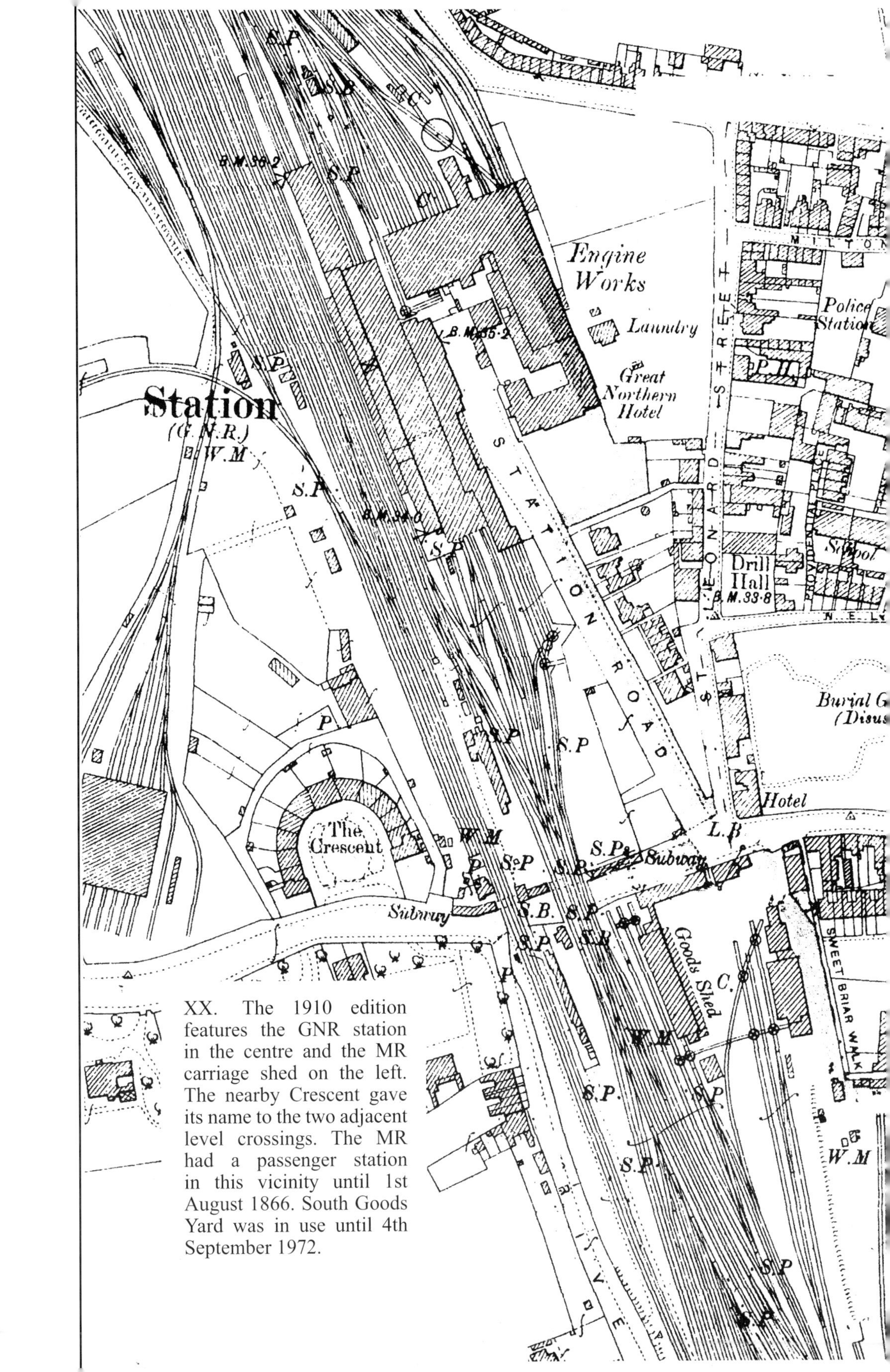

XX. The 1910 edition features the GNR station in the centre and the MR carriage shed on the left. The nearby Crescent gave its name to the two adjacent level crossings. The MR had a passenger station in this vicinity until 1st August 1866. South Goods Yard was in use until 4th September 1972.

51. The MR depot was called Spital Bridge and was north of the station. The shed was within the Eastern Region from 1950 until closure, when it was coded 31F. It had 43 locomotives allocated in 1950 and 34 when it closed on 1st August 1960. It had been 35C until 1958. We witness coaling on 7th May 1927, with staff on and behind the tender of M&GNR no. 7. Coal is stacked and cranes are ready, under the roof. Spital was once an abbreviation for hospital. (H.C.Casserley)

52. This is the MR station mentioned in caption XX and it is to the left of the goods shed. The western span of Crescent Bridge is evident; it was built in 1913 above the western subway shown on the map. The photo is from 1938. (H.C.Casserley)

53. We are north of the station on 20th May 1938 and can see class 2P 4-4-0 ex-MR no. 430, with an officer's inspection saloon. They are on the ex-MR line from Stamford. (H.C.Casserley)

Albums to feature this station include *Peterborough to Newark*, *Peterborough to Kings Lynn*, *Hitchin to Peterborough*, *Peterborough to Lincoln*, *Northampton to Peterborough*, *Branch Lines around March* **and** *Branch Lines around Wisbech*.

54. We move to 25th June 1955 and the new mechanised ash loading plant comes into view. Fully loaded with coal is class 2P 4-4-0 no. 40364, ex-MR. The station had the suffix NORTH from 1st July 1923 to 6th June 1966. The same dates apply to EAST. (H.C.Casserley)

55. In the late 1970s, the station was totally rebuilt and most running lines were repositioned to allow the speed limit to be increased from 20mph to 100. The official reopening was on 30th September 1980. New platforms for March trains, numbered 6 and 7, were opened on 28th December 2013 and photographed on 26th May 2016. In the view are nos 66542 and 170398. (M.J.Stretton)

56. Long sloping approaches to the new wide footbridge were provided to give access to trolleys moving mailbags in vast quantities. Further extensive platform alterations were made in 2013. At the new platform 1 on 7th May 2016 is no. 153308, the 16.25 departure for Lincoln. (V.Mitchell)

PETERBOROUGH EAST

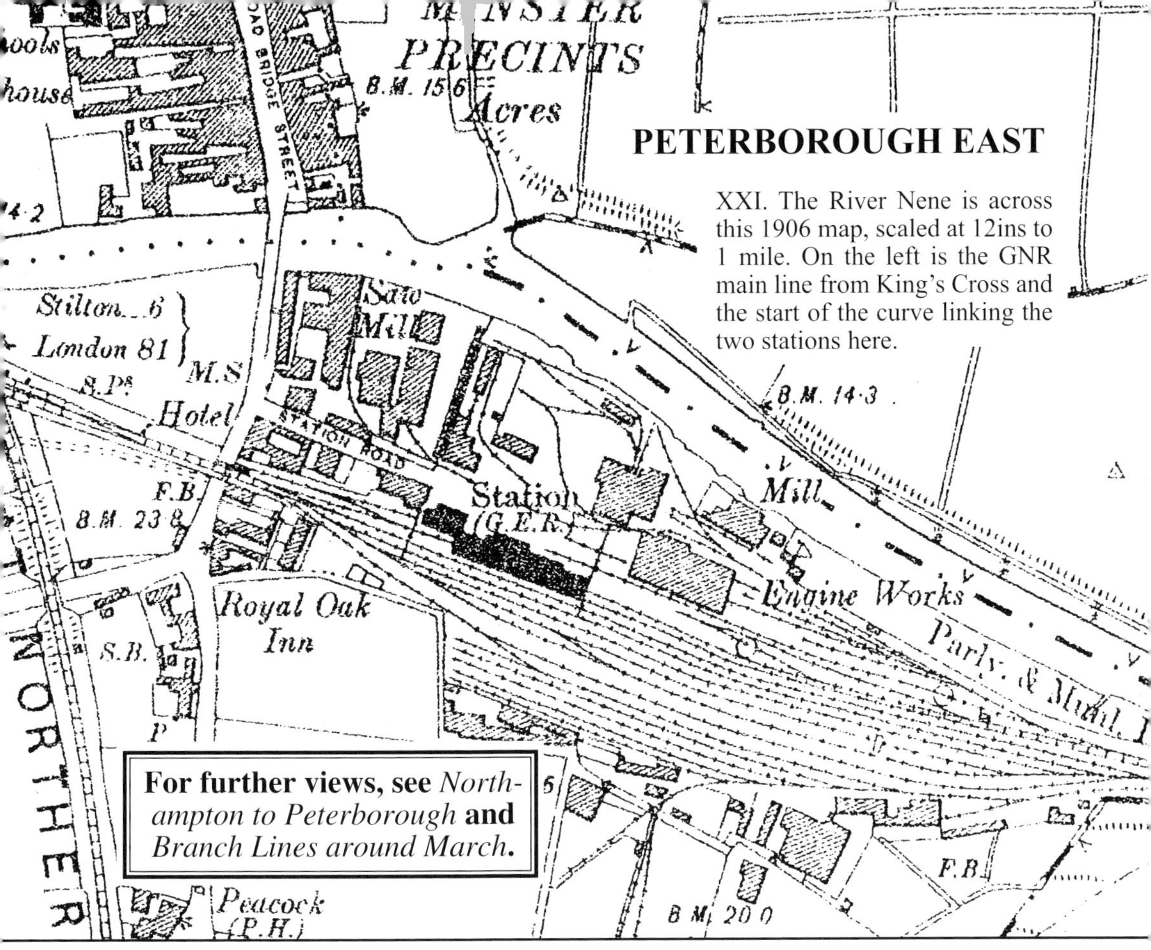

XXI. The River Nene is across this 1906 map, scaled at 12ins to 1 mile. On the left is the GNR main line from King's Cross and the start of the curve linking the two stations here.

For further views, see *Northampton to Peterborough* and *Branch Lines around March*.

57. We make a brief visit here. Most trains from Stamford terminated at Peterborough East in the steam days. The panorama is with a Leicester train in the middle of the picture, headed by 2-6-4T no. 42061 piloting a 4F 0-6-0. On the right is 4-4-0 no. 62536 coupled to empty stock. On the left is a 'Claud Hamilton' class 4-4-0 on station pilot duty. No passenger trains called here after 6th June 1966, but the goods yard was in use until 30th September 1972. Cambridge trains still run through the area. (R.S.Carpenter coll.)

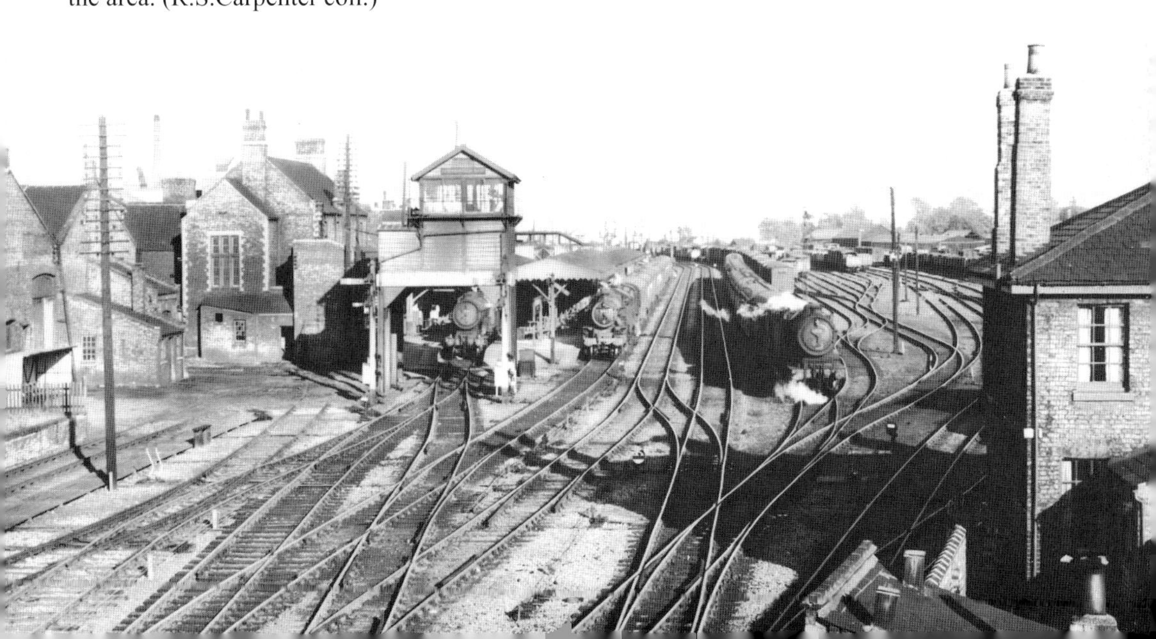

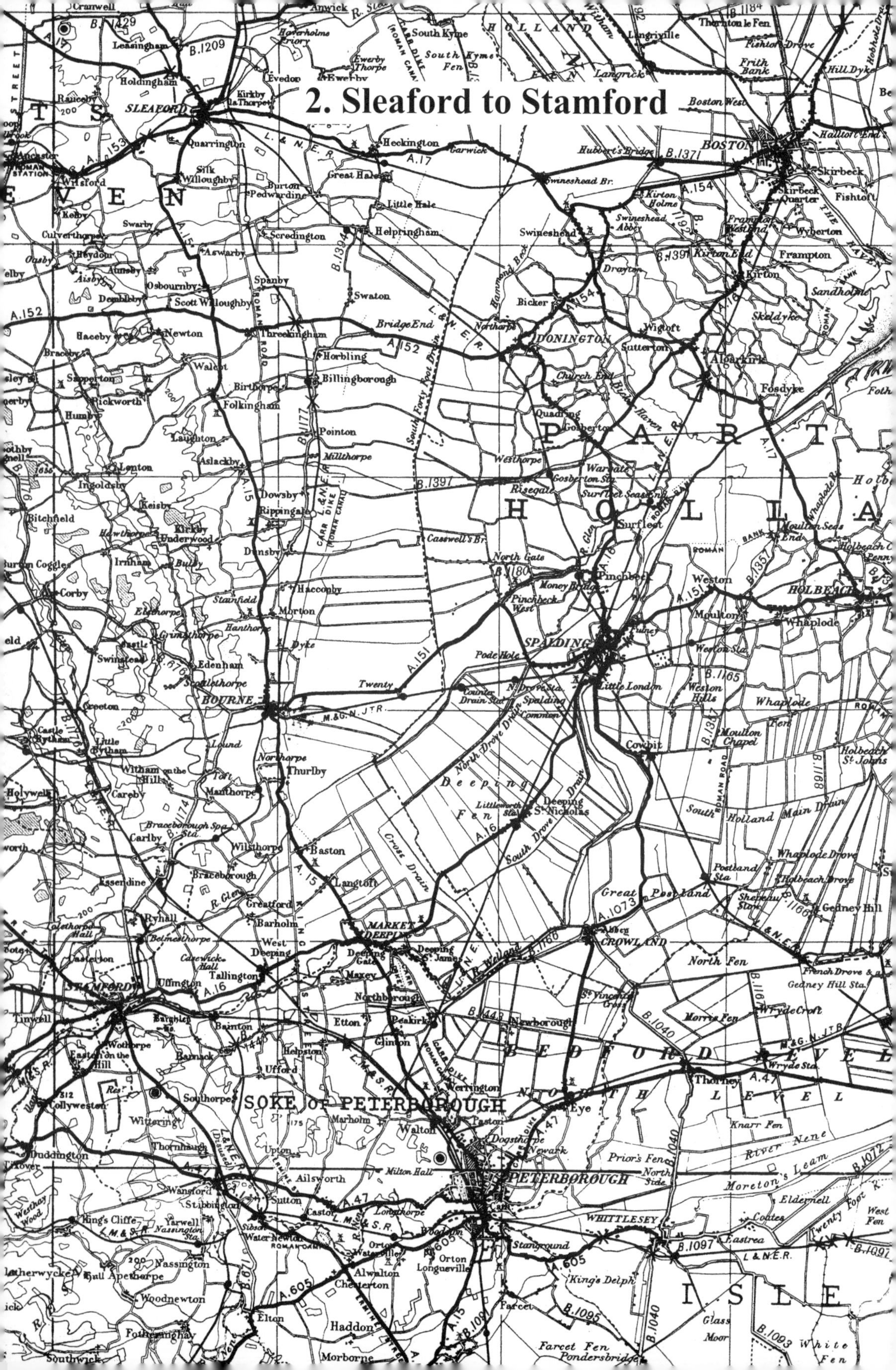
2. Sleaford to Stamford
SLEAFORD
Cranwell
Leasingham
Holdingham
Rauceby
Quarrington
Kirkby la Thorpe
Evedon
Ewerby
Haverholme Priory
South Kyme
South Kyme Fen
Anwick
Heckington
Garwick
Great Hale
Little Hale
Burton Pedwardine
Silk Willoughby
Wilsford
Ancaster
Kelby
Culverthorpe
Heydour
Swarby
Aswarby
Scredington
Helpringham
Swaton
Spanby
Osbournby
Aunsby
Dembleby
Scott Willoughby
Threekingham
Newton
Haceby
Braceby
Sapperton
Pickworth
Walcot
Birthorpe
Folkingham
Horbling
Billingborough
Pointon
Millthorpe
Laughton
Aslackby
Lenton
Ingoldsby
Keisby
Dowsby
Rippingale
Kirkby Underwood
Bitchfield
Irnham
Bulby
Dunsby
Corby
Hacconby
Stainfield
Morton
Elsthorpe
Hanthorpe
Grimsthorpe
Swinstead
Edenham
Scottlethorpe
Dyke
BOURNE
Twenty
Creeton
Castle Bytham
Little Bytham
Lound
Northorpe
Thurlby
Witham on the Hill
Toft
Manthorpe
Careby
Holywell
Carlby
Braceborough Spa Sta.
Wilsthorpe
Baston
Braceborough
Langtoft
Essendine
R. Glen
Greatford
Barholm
Ryhall
Belmesthorpe
West Deeping
MARKET DEEPING
Deeping Gate
Deeping St. James
Maxey
Casewick Hall
Tallington
Uffington
STAMFORD
Tinwell
Barnack
Bainton
Etton
Peakirk
Northborough
Glinton
Helpston
Ufford
Easton on the Hill
Wothorpe
Collyweston
Southorpe
Wittering
Thornhaugh
SOKE OF PETERBOROUGH
Marholm
Walton
Werrington
Paston
Dogsthorpe
Newark
Upton
Milton Hall
Ailsworth
PETERBOROUGH
Duddington
Wansford
Stibbington
Sutton
Castor
Longthorpe
King's Cliffe
Yarwell
Nassington
Water Newton
Orton Waterville
Orton Longueville
Alwalton
Chesterton
Woodston
Stanground
Apethorpe
Woodnewton
Elton
Fotheringhay
Haddon
Morborne
Farcet
Farcet Fen
Pondersbridge
Southwick
Boston West
BOSTON
Hubbert's Bridge
Swineshead Br.
Swineshead
Swineshead Abbey
Kirton Holme
Skirbeck
Skirbeck Quarter
Fishtoft
Frampton West End
Wyberton
Frampton
Kirton End
Kirton
Drayton
Bicker
Northorpe
DONINGTON
Wigtoft
Sutterton
Algarkirk
Fosdyke
Church End
Quadring
Gosberton
Westhorpe
Wargate
Gosberton Sta.
Risegate
Surfleet
Bridge End
Caswell's Br.
North Gate
Pinchbeck
Pinchbeck West
Money Bridge
Weston
Moulton
Whaplode
HOLBEACH
SPALDING
Pode Hole
Little London
Weston Hills
Cowbit
Moulton Chapel
Deeping Fen
Deeping St. Nicholas
Littleworth Sta.
South Drove Drain
North Drove Drain
Spalding Common
Cross Drain
Great Postland
Postland Sta.
Whaplode Drove
Holbeach Drove
Gedney Hill
CROWLAND
North Fen
French Drove & Gedney Hill Sta.
Morris Fen
Wryde Croft
Newborough
St. Vincent's Cross
Eye
Thorney
Wryde Sta.
Knarr Fen
River Nene
Morton's Leam
Prior's Fen
North Side
WHITTLESEY
Eastrea
Coates
Eldernell
King's Delph
Glass Moor
White Fen
Twenty Foot R.
Langrick
Langriville
Thornton le Fen
Fishtoft Drove
Frith Bank
Hill Dyke
Sandholme
Skeldyke
Moulton Seas End
Holbeach St. Johns
South Holland Main Drain
Whaplode Fen
K E S T E V E N
H O L L A N D
P A R T S   O F   H O L L A N D
B E D F O R D   L E V E L
N O R T H   L E V E L
I S L E

SLEAFORD

58. We look west in 1961 and see the six-siding goods yard on the left. The cattle pens were at the southern border of the yard. The other sidings, crane and goods shed are obscured by the main buildings. The yard closed on 8th July 1991, with the end of Speedlink, and the shed was demolished in 2003. East Box had a 50-lever frame and is a listed structure, controlling lifting barriers. It had a panel from 2011. North and South boxes closed on 14th April 2014. (Stations UK)

Other views can be enjoyed in
Nottingham to Boston; **pictures nos 91 to 98.**

← XXII. The 1946 edition of the ¼ in to 1 mile map has Ketton and the line onwards lower left; Sleaford and the Cranwell branch top left. The route to Spalding and Murrow runs southeast from there, across the Levels. The line to Bourne and Stamford runs south.

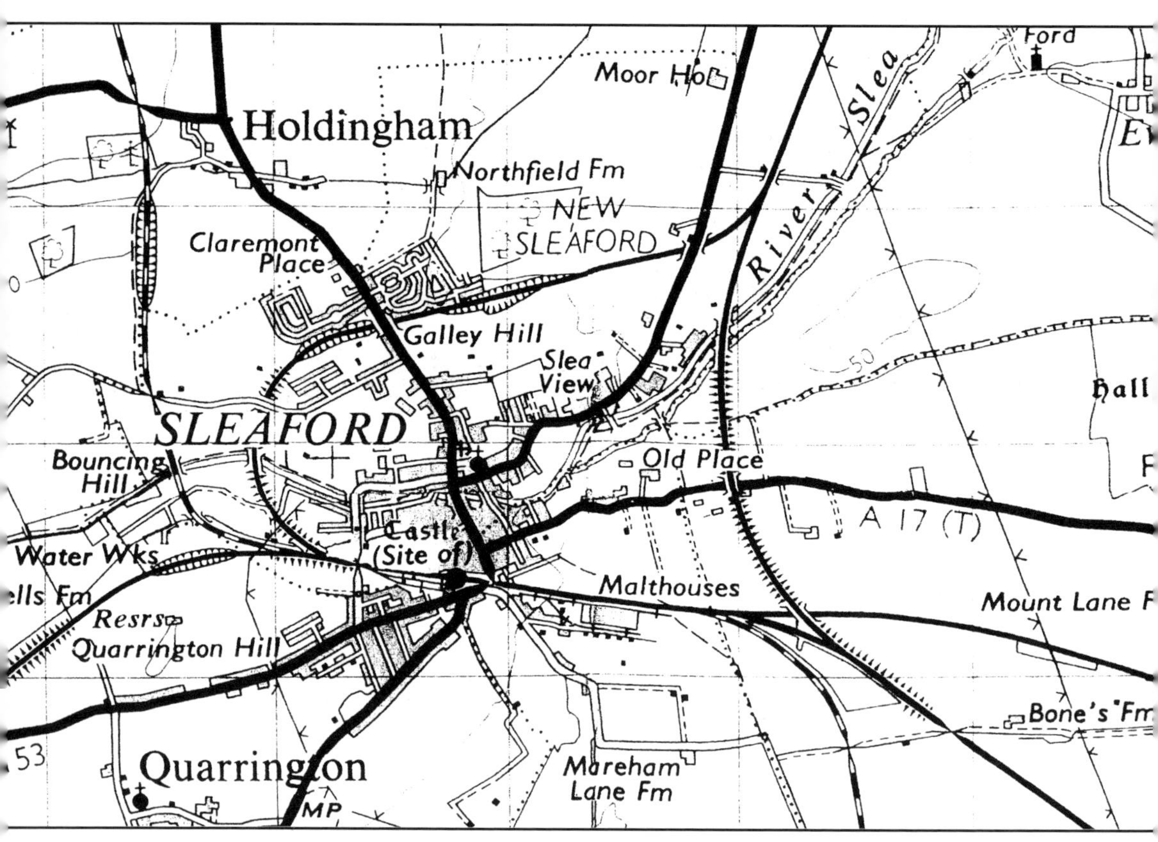

XXIII. The 1946 edition at 2ins to 1 mile clarifies the connections. Regard the station as at the centre of a clock and at 1.0pm you have the route to Lincoln, 3.15 to Boston, 4.0 to Spalding, 5.30 to Bourne and 8.0 to Grantham. The connecting link east of the town was closed from around 1985 and reopened in 2013. Top left is the single track to RAF Cranwell.

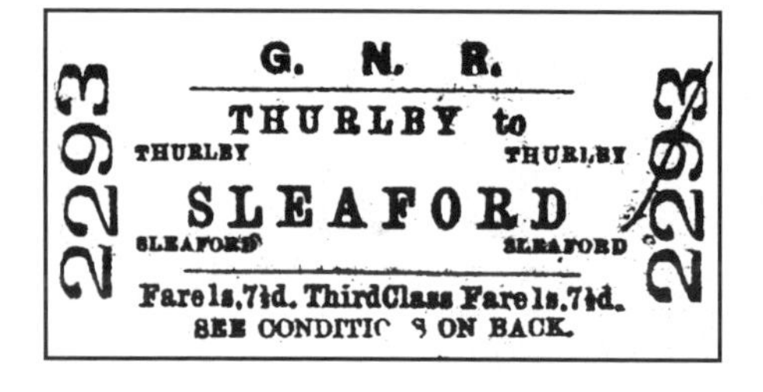

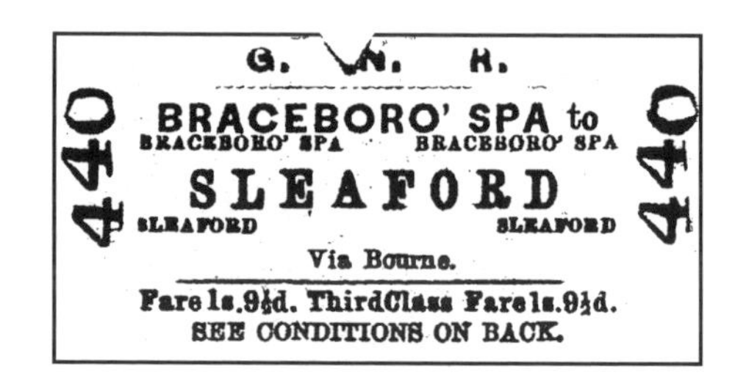

ASWARBY & SCREDINGTON

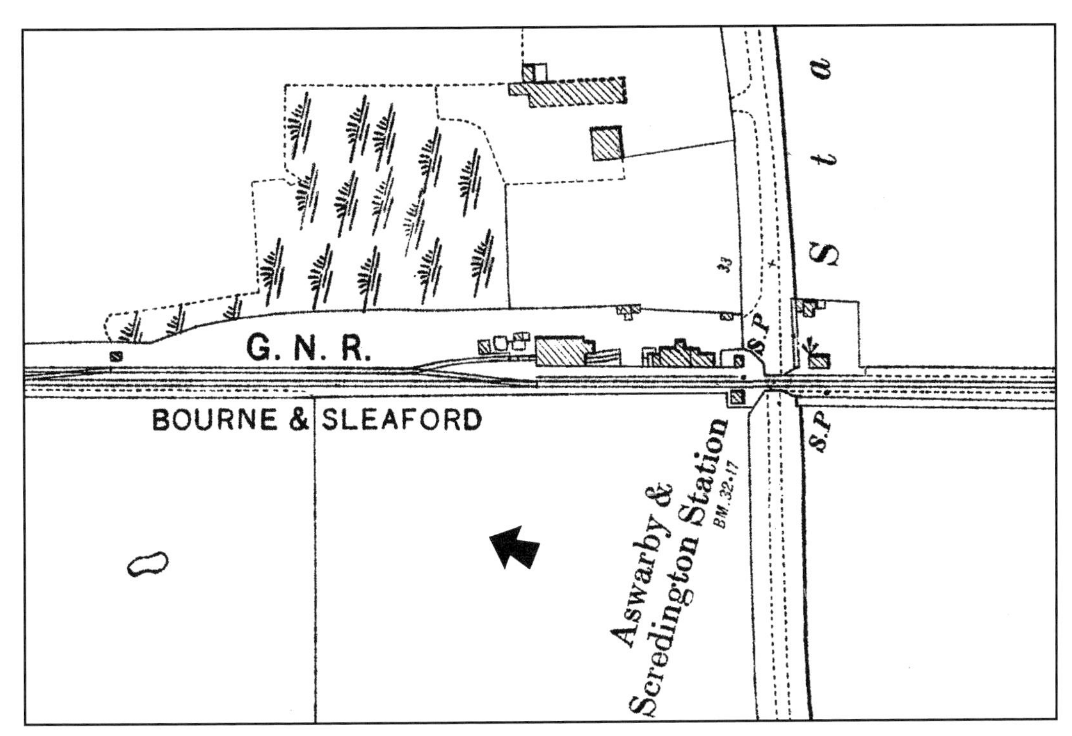

XXIV. Aswarby had 120 residents in 1901, while its neighbour had 285. The first name had been added on 1st February 1875. The 15-lever box was in use from 1891 to 1931. The 1904 map has a brick and tile works at the top. It would have generated coal in and products out of the goods yard.

59. The station opened on 2nd January 1870, but closed with the line to Bourne on 22nd September 1930. The yard was in use until 28th July 1956. The northward photograph is from 18th May 1959. (Milepost 92½)

BILLINGBOROUGH & HORBLING

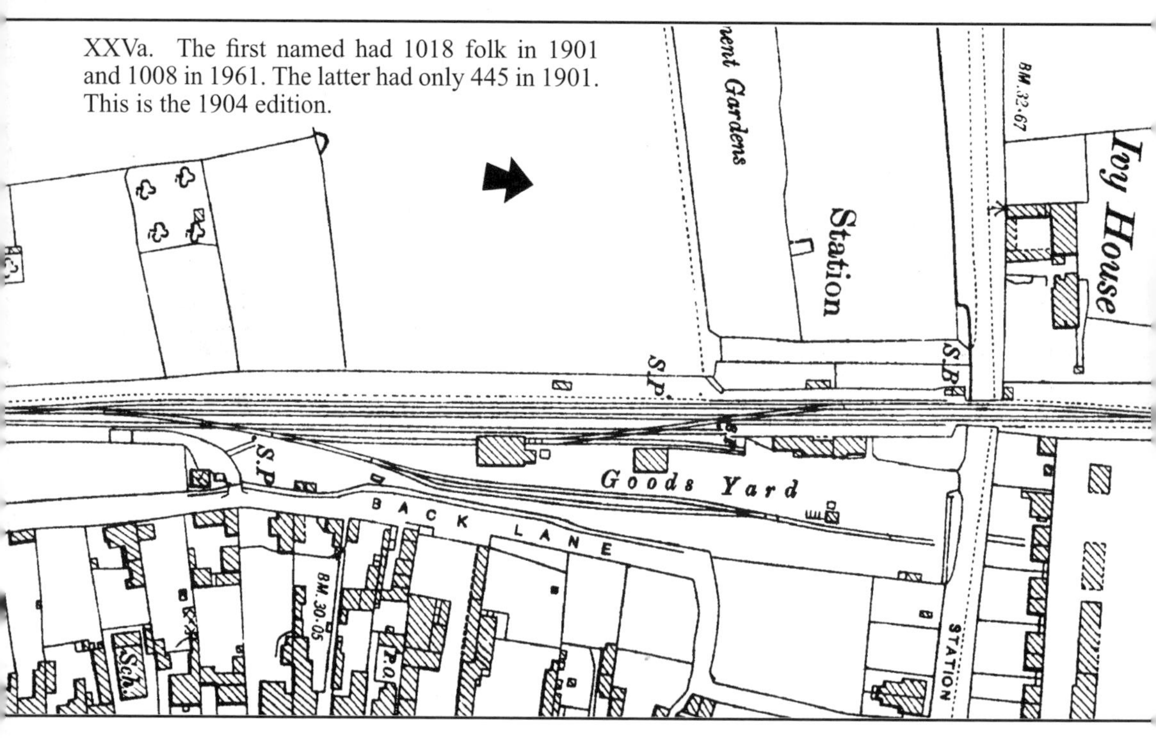

XXVa. The first named had 1018 folk in 1901 and 1008 in 1961. The latter had only 445 in 1901. This is the 1904 edition.

60. A northward postcard view includes the 20-lever 1891 North Box, which was closed on 28th February 1959. South Box (see map XXVb) also had 20 levers, but closed on 28th July 1956. Further south was Millthorpe Siding, which had an 8-lever ground frame. (P.Laming coll.)

61. The station was built on arches because of the soft ground. It closed on 22nd September 1930, but goods traffic continued until 15th June 1964. However, this ceased northwards on 28th July 1956. (P.Laming coll.)

XXVb. The 1949 issue at 6ins to 1 mile is included to show the proximity of the community.

RIPPINGALE

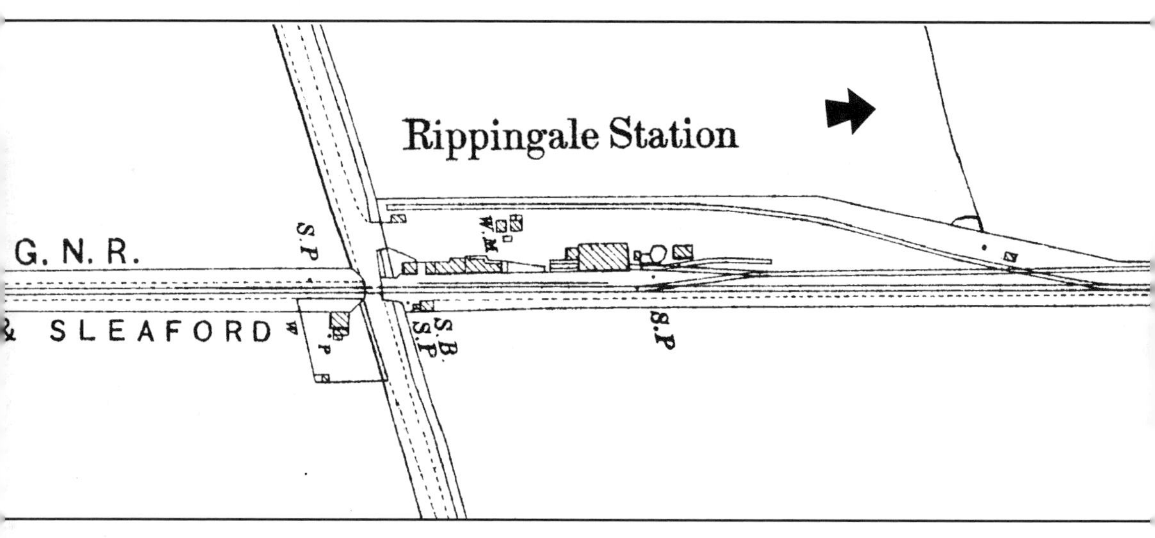

XXVI. The village housed 473 in 1901 and its station is shown on the 1904 edition. They were separated by about one mile.

62. On the right is the 1891 signal box, which closed after the end of passenger services, in 1931. The spacious goods shed was provided with a 30cwt crane. Goods traffic continued here until 15th June 1964. A notable commodity once conveyed were blackcurrants for Ribena manufacture. (P.Laming coll.)

63. This northward panorama is from 3rd October 1959, when the yard gates were still regularly locked. On the right is the accommodation for the level crossing gate keeper. (H.B.Priestley/R.Humm)

64. The buildings and goods shed were up for sale in 2016, together with 1.2 acres of land and a track length bearing 0-4-0ST *Elizabeth*, built in 1922 by Avonside and used at Croydon Gas Works. The track came from a sugar beet factory near Peterborough. (Janet Smith)

MORTON ROAD

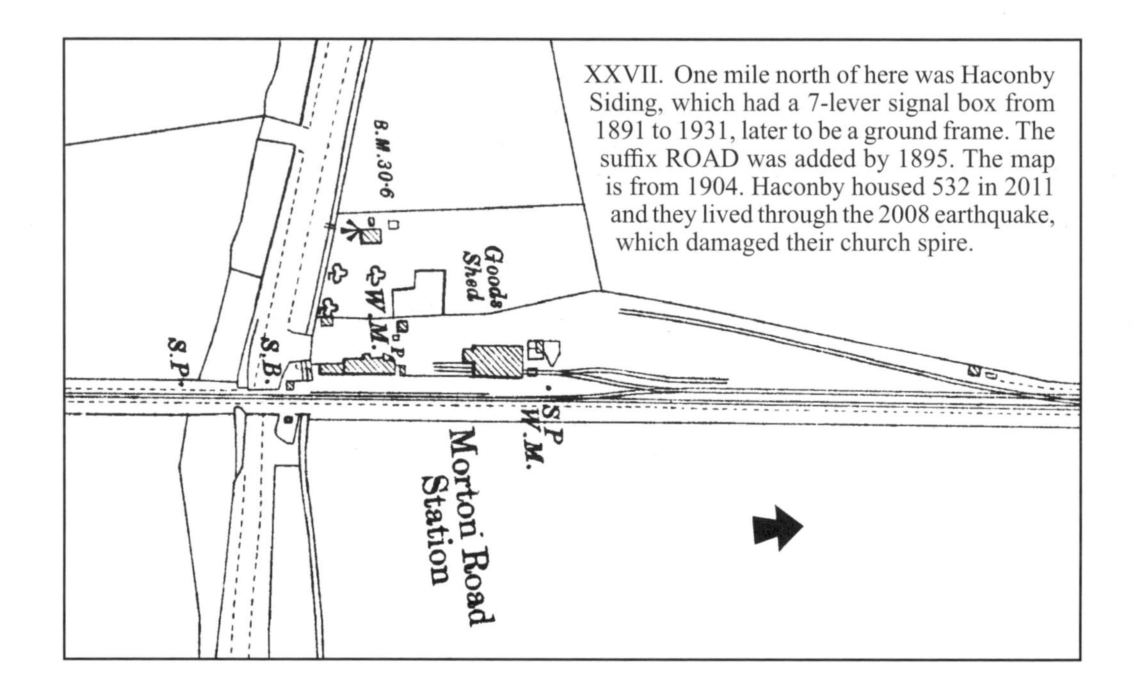

XXVII. One mile north of here was Haconby Siding, which had a 7-lever signal box from 1891 to 1931, later to be a ground frame. The suffix ROAD was added by 1895. The map is from 1904. Haconby housed 532 in 2011 and they lived through the 2008 earthquake, which damaged their church spire.

65. The architectural details and all the dates are as those for the previous station. The 10-lever signal box was to the left of the camera, which was here on 11th February 1961. The site is now covered by a housing development, but the main buildings still stand. (D.A.Thompson/R.Humm)

BOURNE

66. Red Hall is shown at the top of the next map. It is of Elizabethan origin and the GNR was asked not to demolish it. Thus it contained the booking office for many years, but it was later fenced off and a hut was provided for tickets. One of the first two platforms was close to the left of it. (P.Laming coll.)

67. A view from the footbridge, seen in the previous picture, features the 10.01am Saxby to Spalding train, on 27th May 1937. The locomotive is LNER no. 085. It had been built in 1900 for the GNR, but allocated to the M&GNR. The LNER took over the M&GN on 1st October 1936 and simply added '0' in front of the numbers of 12 ageing locos. The signal is a somersault type of GNR origin and beyond it is the turntable and water tower. (H.C.Casserley)

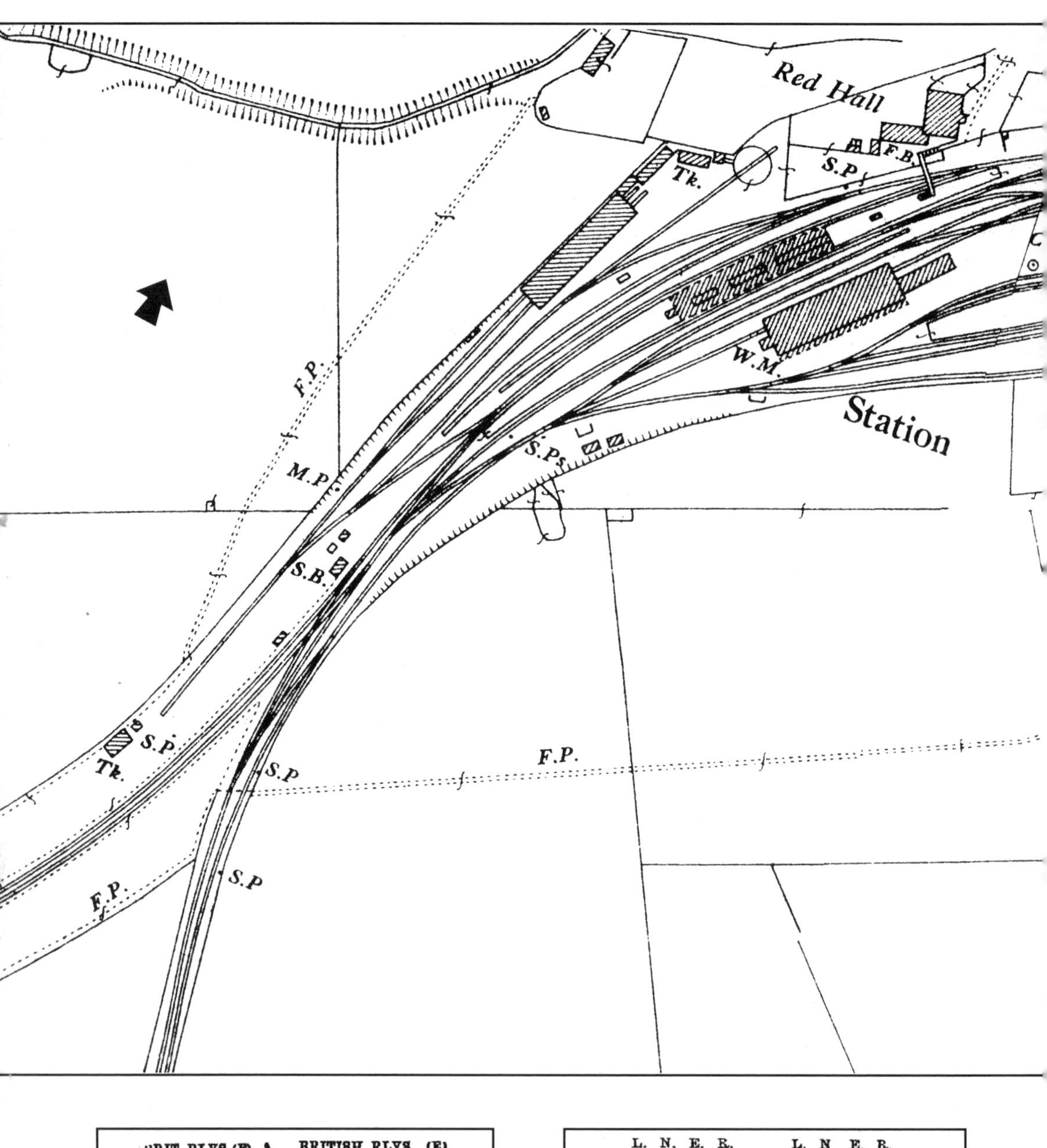

Red Hall
Tk.
S.P
F.B.
W.M.
Station
F.P.
M.P
S.Ps
S.B.
S.P
Tk.
S.P
F.P.
S.P
F.P.

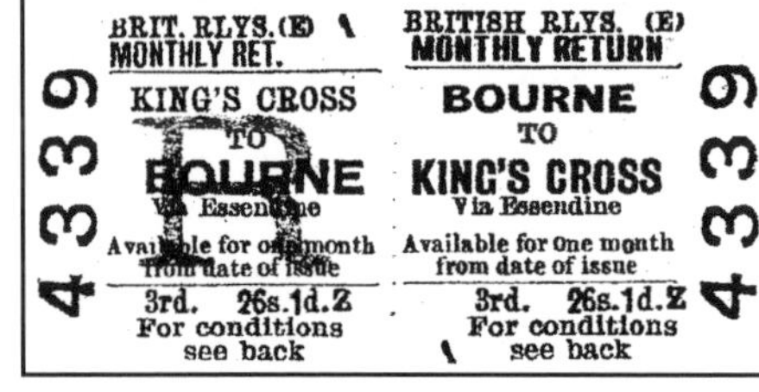

BRIT. RLYS. (E)
MONTHLY RET.
KING'S CROSS
TO
BOURNE
Via Essendine
Available for one month from date of issue
3rd. 26s.1d.Z
For conditions see back
BRITISH RLYS. (E)
MONTHLY RETURN
BOURNE
TO
KING'S CROSS
Via Essendine
Available for one month from date of issue
3rd. 26s.1d.Z
For conditions see back
4339
4339

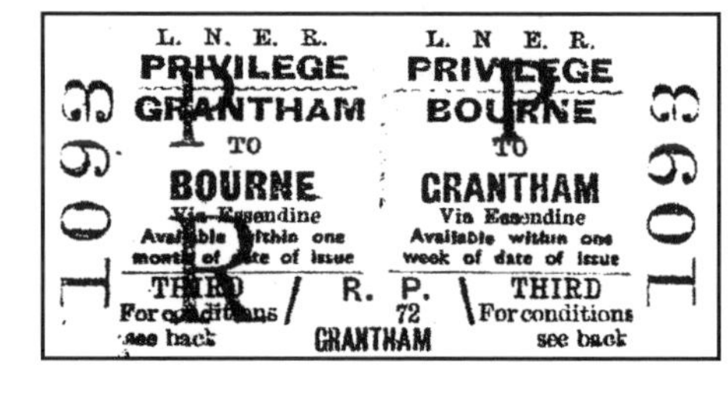

L. N. E. R.
PRIVILEGE
GRANTHAM
TO
BOURNE
Via Essendine
Available within one month of date of issue
THIRD
For conditions see back
L. N. E. R.
PRIVILEGE
BOURNE
TO
GRANTHAM
Via Essendine
Available within one week of date of issue
THIRD
For conditions see back
R. P.
72
GRANTHAM
1093
1093

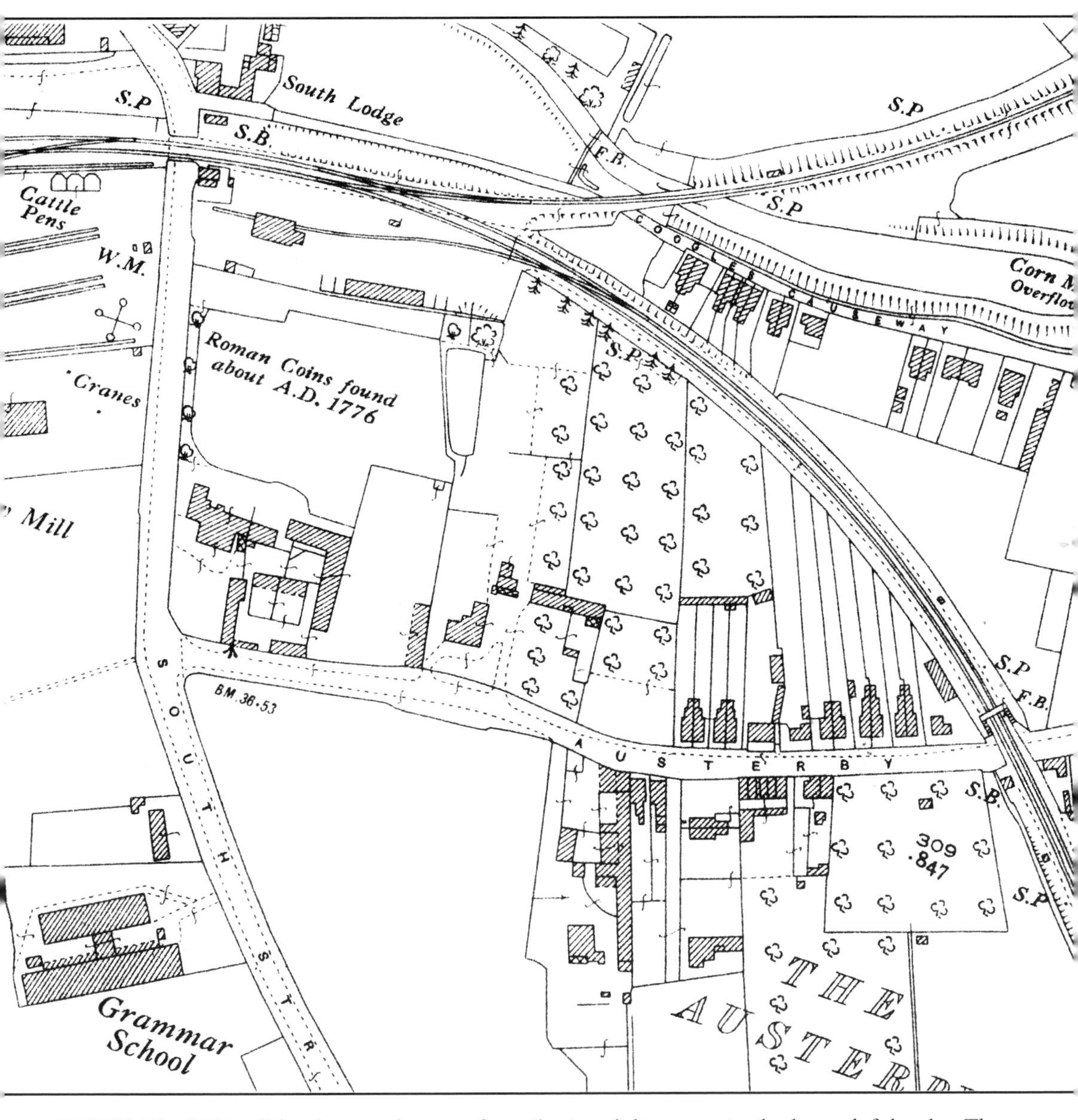

XXVIII. The 1930 edition has our journey from the top right corner to the lower left border. The line on the left served Kingston's Siding for their brickworks and then continued to Saxby. Lower right is the route to Spalding. The railway crane shown was rated at 10 tons. East and West signal boxes are on opposite pages. Both had 45 levers and closed on 28th February 1959.

68. Seen on the same day is no. 404, a class 2P 4-4-0, ex-MR. These fine machines were built in 1882-1901. The train is the 6.40pm to Nottingham. The top floor of the goods shed acted as a warehouse for customers. There had once been a regular overnight van of watercress to London. (H.C.Casserley)

69. We move forward to 12th May 1956 to examine the engine shed, which is on the left page of the map. It was GNR property and was lengthened in 1898. Closure came in 1953. (R.M.Casserley)

70. Seen on the same day is class 2P 4-4-0 no. 40504 on the 60ft turntable. The original one was only 45ft long. Red Hall appears in this photograph and the next. (R.M.Casserley)

See *Branch Lines around Spalding* pictures 11 to 22 for further details.

71. The final shot from that day is a fine panorama featuring all the structures mentioned and includes the island platform, which carried the waiting room and the toilet facilities. (R.M.Casserley)

72. This undated view gives a fine profile of class 2P 4-4-0 no. 40542 departing with an express for the Midlands. The goods yard remained in use until 5th April 1965. (W.A.Camwell/SLS)

73. It is 28th February 1959 and the last Spalding to Birmingham express was unusually adorned. The headboard travelled to Leicester and back. Here it is carried by class 4MT 2-6-0 no. 43060. (M.J.Stretton)

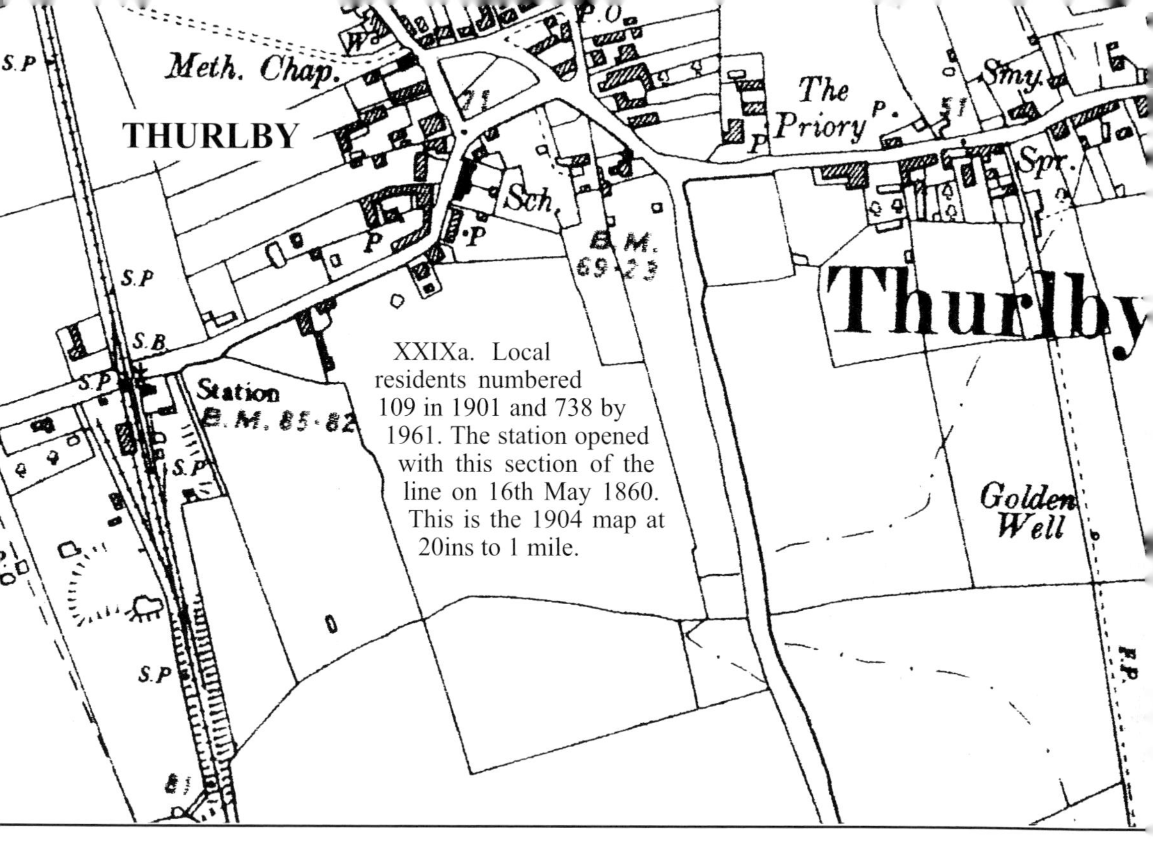

XXIXa. Local residents numbered 109 in 1901 and 738 by 1961. The station opened with this section of the line on 16th May 1860. This is the 1904 map at 20ins to 1 mile.

74. The lofty signal box of 1891 became a ground frame in 1926 and closed with the line on 18th June 1951. On the right is the gate to the goods yard, which was on a loop line, seen in the foreground. Sugar beet had once been loaded here in large quantities. (P.Laming coll.)

75. Only the platform on the right was in use. The other line passed through the goods shed, which had a 30cwt crane. The site became a highways depot. The ground disc shows 7, which is the lever number. It rotated 180°; it now shows clear. (R.Humm coll.)

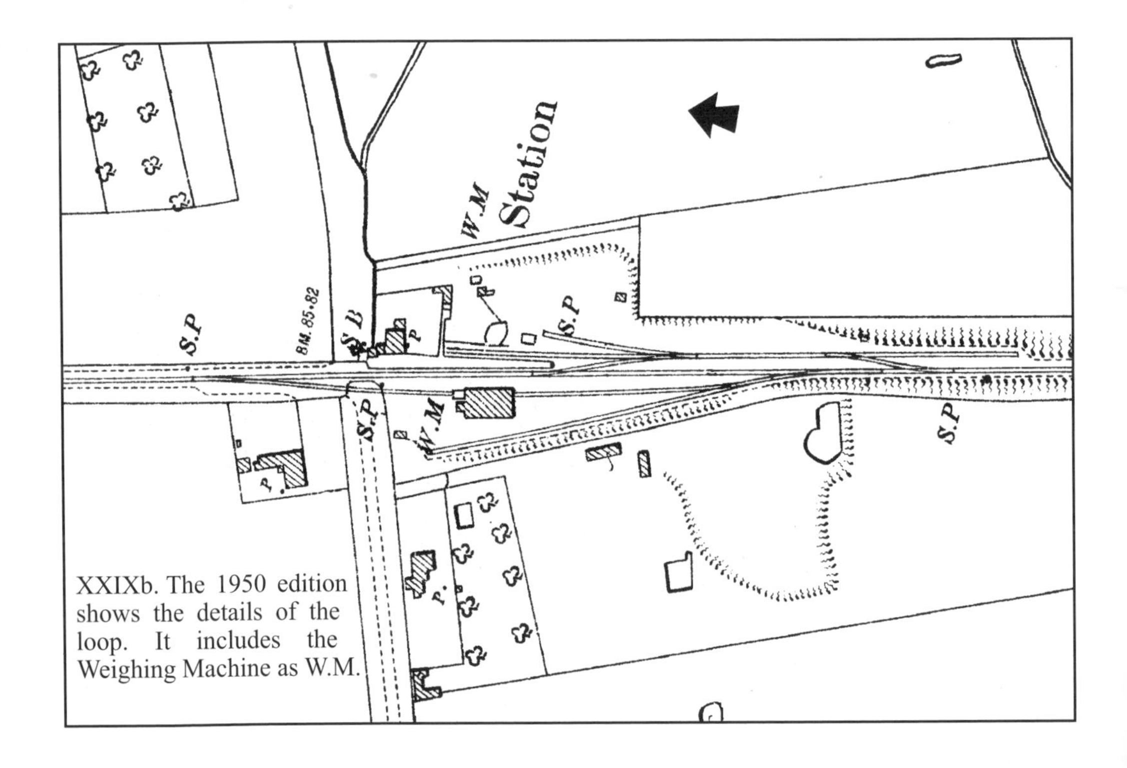

XXIXb. The 1950 edition shows the details of the loop. It includes the Weighing Machine as W.M.

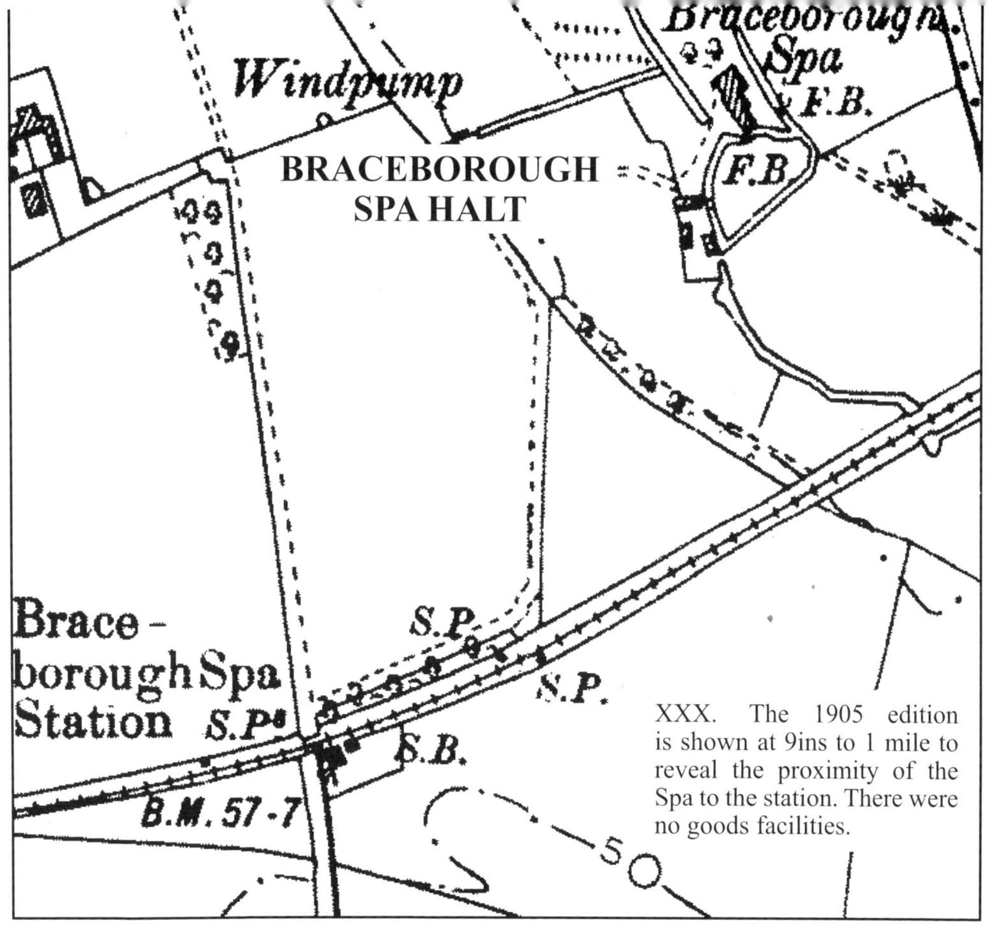

XXX. The 1905 edition is shown at 9ins to 1 mile to reveal the proximity of the Spa to the station. There were no goods facilities.

76. The station opened with the line and became a halt on 19th February 1934, which meant that staffing ceased. This eastward view was featured on a postcard in around 1900. The 1890 signal box lasted until 1934. Spa water was dispatched by train for many years, much to a pharmacy at 50 Wigmore Street in the West End of London. The Spa closed in 1930. The station was sold as a dwelling in 1968. The village was ¾ mile southeastwards. (P.Laming coll.)

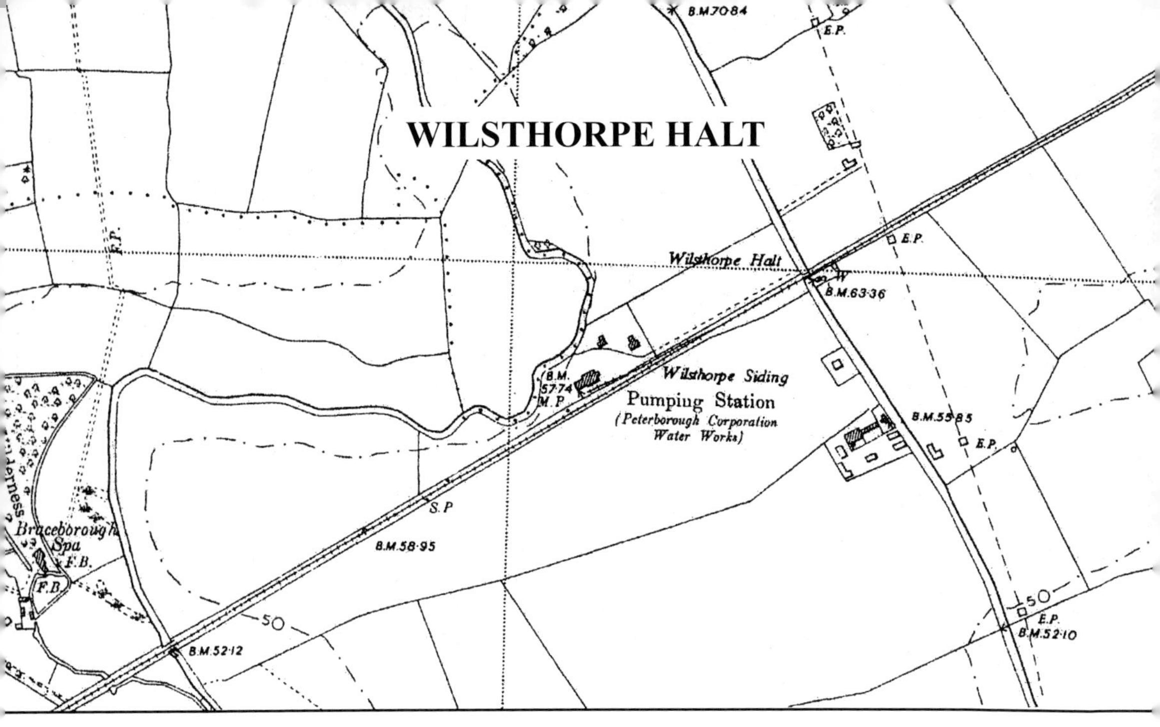

XXXI. The Spa is lower left on this 1951 extract at 6ins to 1 mile. It is included to show Wilsthorpe Halt, which was open from 1st December 1933 until 18th June 1951. It was Wilsthorpe Crossing on most documents, but HALT was on the sign board. The siding was used mostly for coal for the water pumps. E.P. refers to Electricity Pylons and 50 is the number of feet above sea level.

77. No platform was provided and so passengers had to use the steps on the train. The guard attended to the lamp. (M.Black)

ESSENDINE

XXXII. The 1916 edition has the quadruple track of the East Coast Main Line of the GNR across it. Curving lower right is our route from Sleaford and Bourne. Trains ran into the up bay. We will depart south on the line nearest the gas works. The latter was GNR property and supplied the station's needs.

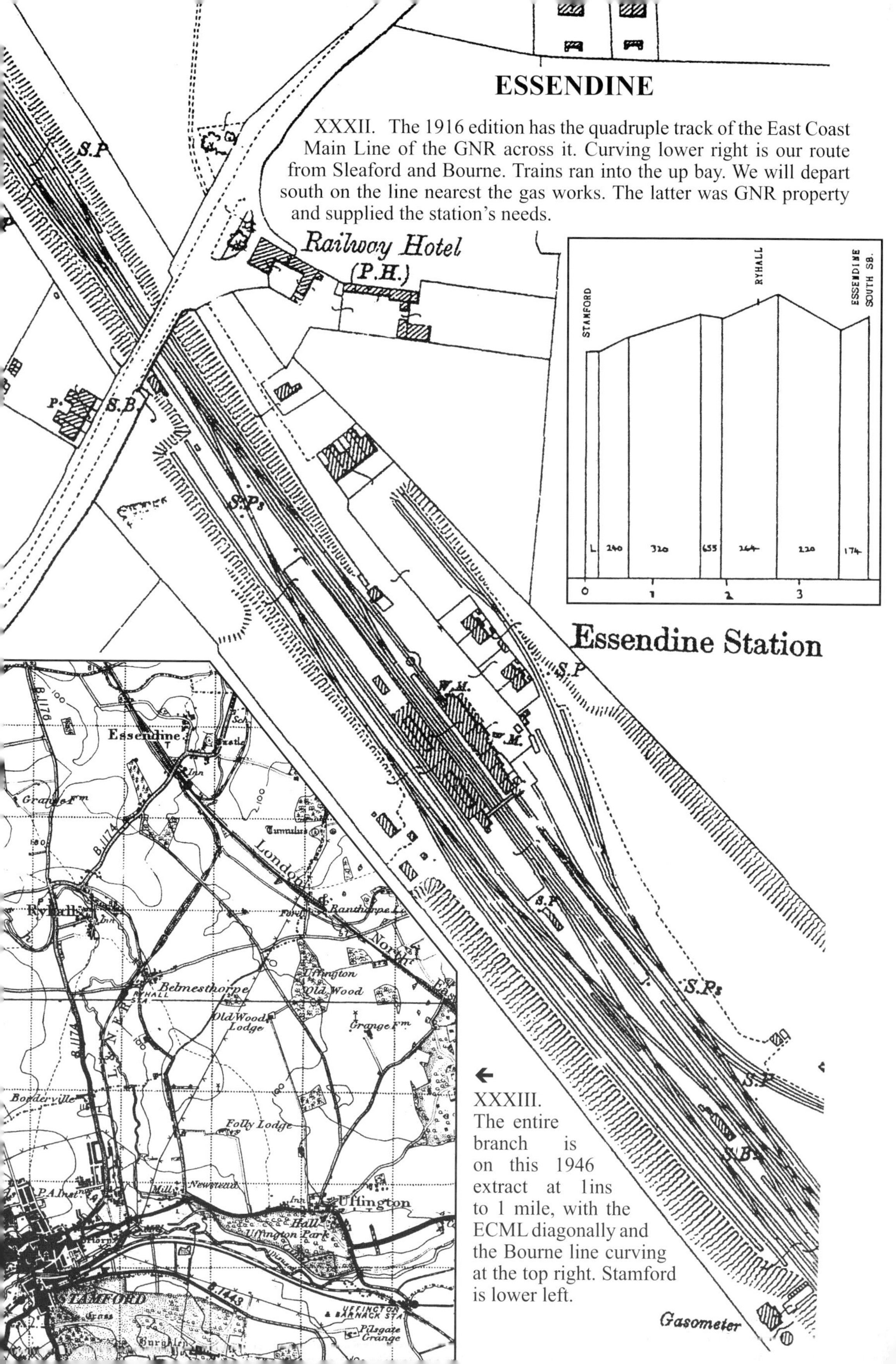

← XXXIII. The entire branch is on this 1946 extract at 1ins to 1 mile, with the ECML diagonally and the Bourne line curving at the top right. Stamford is lower left.

78. Here we have the station, the east elevation and part of the footbridge. In the distance is the 1883 South Box. It had 105 levers and was in use until 21st December 1964. The station closed to passengers on 15th June 1959 and to goods on 7th March 1966. (P.Laming coll.)

79. North Box is in this northward view from August 1952. It had a 55-lever frame, which was worked from 1912 until 13th April 1975. North of here was the route on which the world speed record for a steam locomotive was achieved on 3rd July 1938 by LNER class A4 4-6-2 no. 4468 *Mallard*. (P.Kingston)

80. Waiting on the west side of the island platform on 13th September 1954 is class C12 4-4-2T no. 67365. It is working the 12.52pm to Stamford East. The branch was closed briefly in 1935, due to bridge brickwork falling. (R.J.Buckley/SLS)

81. A branch train is arriving from Stamford on 7th July 1956 behind class C12 no. 67394. Much agricultural equipment was manufactured in the district. The tall items on the right appear to be hay elevators. (B.W.Ware/R.S.Carpenter)

RYHALL & BELMESTHORPE

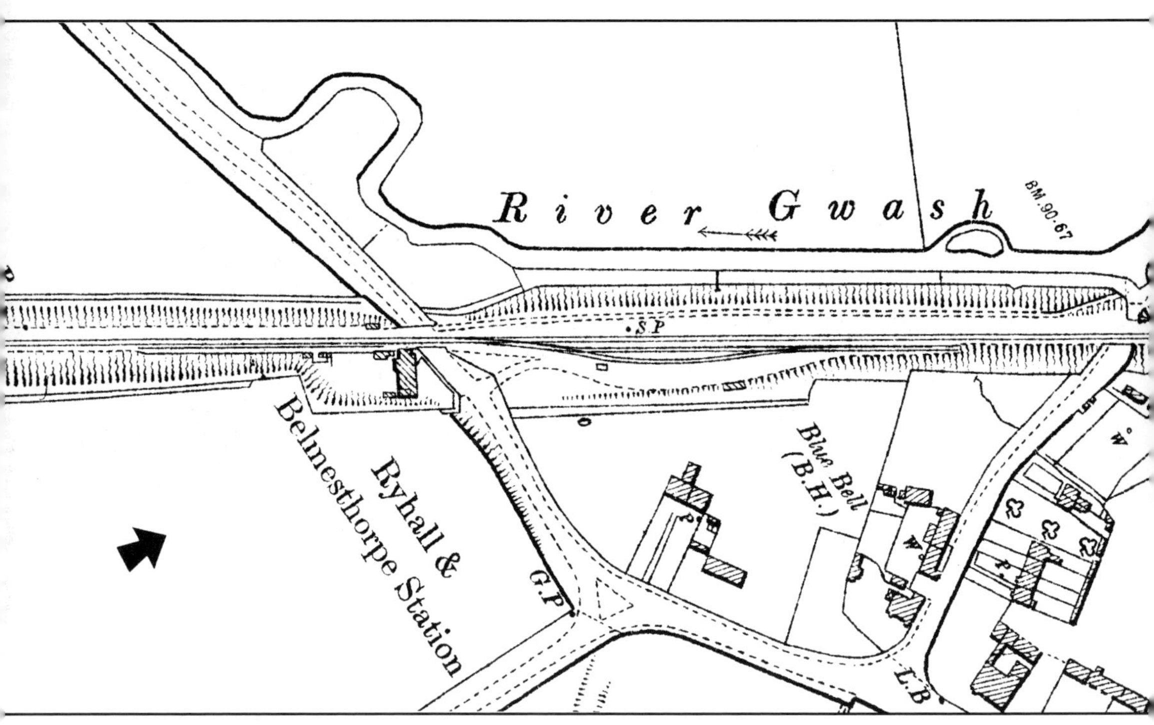

XXXIV. The 1904 edition reveals that the river had to be realigned to allow the construction of a straight embankment. Note that the bridges were built to accommodate double track.

82. A hut protected the 9-lever frame, which was in use from 1887 until 15th June 1959, when the branch closed. The village of Ryhall housed 582 souls in 1901 and 1052 in 1961. The station was noted for its displays of primroses seasonally. (W.A.Camwell/SLS)

83. Eldred's Lime Siding was south of here in 1938, but the siding on the map was not listed. A coal wagon and a loading gauge are evident on 21st April 1958. Goods facilities lasted until branch closure. (R.M.Casserley)

84. Seen on 14th April 1959 is class N5 0-6-2T no. 69322 with the 5.55pm Essendine to Stamford service. The start of the siding can be seen, as can the additional parcel store in the form of a van body. The overflowing injector was of no benefit to the line's floral display. (H.C.Casserley)

3. Stamford to Wansford

XXXV. The 1946 map at 1ins to 1 mile has the single track from Essendine at the top border and the closed Wansford line almost reaching the lower border. Having shut in 1929, this appears to be the limit of track lifting. Uffington is illustrated in pictures 44-46. Road numbers were allocated in 1919; the A1 and A16 are noted here.

➔ XXXVI. Before entering the station, trains passed the private sidings of Martin's Cultivator Co. and Blackstone & Co., later to be Rutland Engineering Works. The lower inset is the area diagram from *The Railway Magazine* of 1946. Blackstones produced submarine parts in WWI and generated much extra traffic. Its sidings lasted as Priory Siding until 27th November 1967. The ex-GNR route east of the terminus is now part of the Torpel Way path.

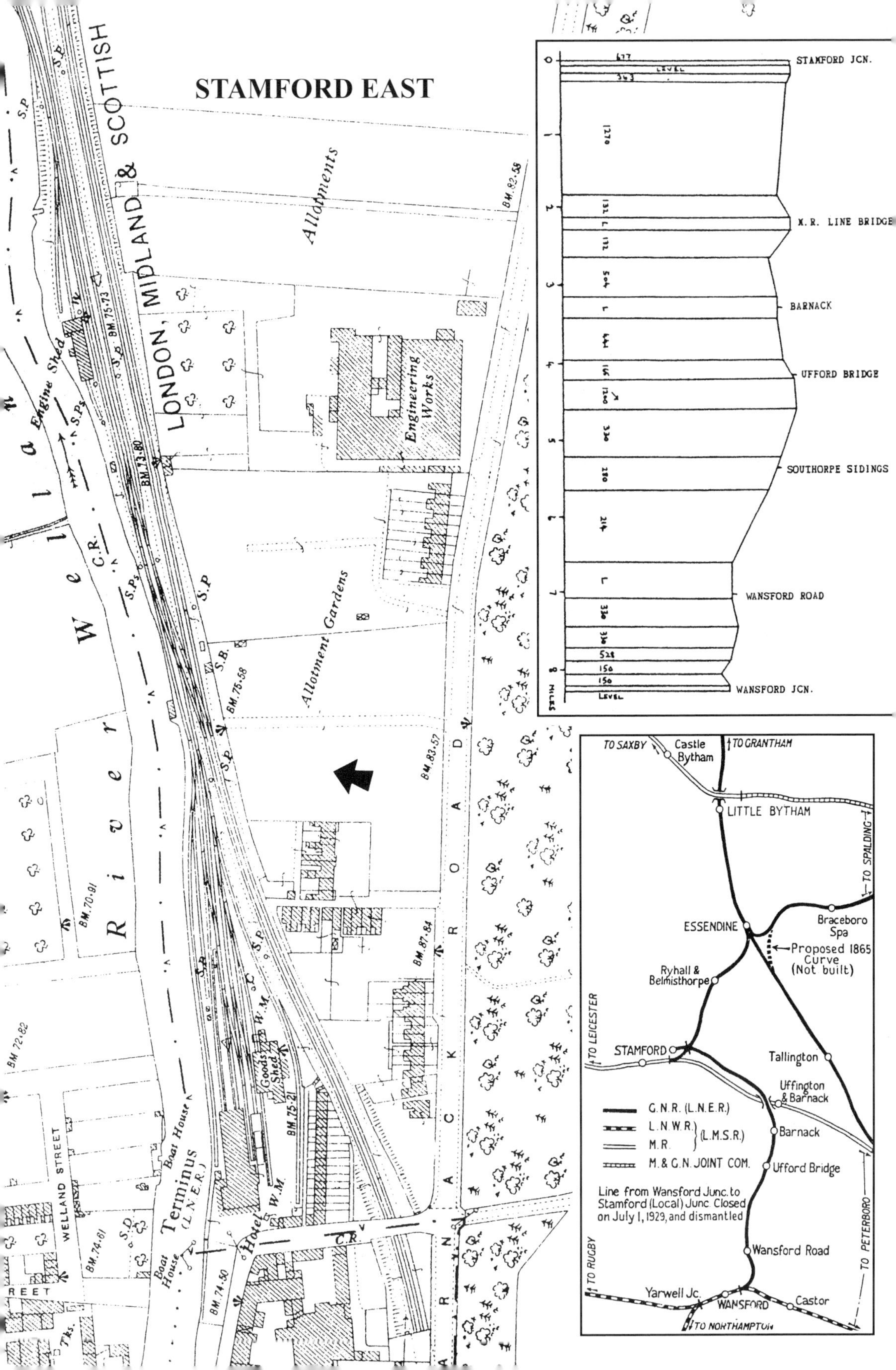
STAMFORD EAST
LONDON, MIDLAND & SCOTTISH
Allotments
Engineering Works
Allotment Gardens
Engine Shed
River Welland
Goods Shed
Terminus (L.N.E.R.)
Boat House
Hotel
WELLAND STREET
RYHALL ROAD
STAMFORD JCN.
M.R. LINE BRIDGE
BARNACK
UFFORD BRIDGE
SOUTHORPE SIDINGS
WANSFORD ROAD
WANSFORD JCN.
MILES
LEVEL
TO SAXBY
Castle Bytham
TO GRANTHAM
LITTLE BYTHAM
TO SPALDING
ESSENDINE
Braceboro Spa
Proposed 1865 Curve (Not built)
Ryhall & Belmisthorpe
TO LEICESTER
STAMFORD
Tallington
Uffington & Barnack
Barnack
Ufford Bridge
G.N.R. (L.N.E.R.)
L.N.W.R.
M.R.
(L.M.S.R.)
M. & G.N. JOINT COM.
Line from Wansford Junc. to Stamford (Local) Junc. Closed on July 1, 1929, and dismantled
Wansford Road
TO RUGBY
Yarwell Jc.
WANSFORD
Castor
TO NORTHAMPTON
TO PETERBORO

85. We start our survey of this splendid station with three Edwardian postcard views. Two GNR locos are present; left is class J23 0-6-0T no. 161 and right is no. 195, a class J5 0-6-0. (LOSA)

86. Here we look across the River Welland at the station's frontage, which was aptly on Water Street. This name was used as a suffix from 1867 to 1939 by Bradshaw. Flooding was not uncommon here. Goods stock stands in the siding, while a loco waits on a departing train. (LOSA)

87. An arrival stands on the right, while a departure is adjacent. Note that the platform has been lengthened (in 1896) and that the massive goods shed is on the left. Gas for the lights was produced immediately north of the river bridge, but the coal for it came by water. (LOSA)

88. We can now enjoy three pictures from August 1952. Barrows are ready for passenger train parcel traffic. Charges were higher for this, but speed was greater. The smoke ducts are shown in detail. The platform on the left was usually for Wansford and the right one for Essendine. (P.Kingston)

89. The position of the Albert Footbridge is evident in this westward view. Until 1909, the station toilets discharged direct into the river, but they were then connected to the town's sewers. The end of one smoke duct is visible. (P.Kingston)

90. Ex-GNR class C12 4-4-2T no. 67361 is shunting, as two men complete a movement while the shunter stands with his pole. The main shed still stands, but the office extension was demolished to allow for residential development. The nearby crane was rated at 6-ton capacity. (P.Kingston)

91. A corner of the impressive booking hall was photographed in 1945. Described as of Elizabethan character with mullioned windows, the building contains pairs of beams rising from carved corbels. The gallery is on scrolled brackets, supporting a splendid balustrade. (*Railway Magazine*)

92. The signal box on the left is the Midland Railway's Stamford Junction. The principal purpose of the box was to control the Midland end of the crossover to the Great Northern yard. The box was opened in 1882 and abolished in 1957. Its functions were transferred to the GNR Stamford East box. The GN box opened on 14th May 1893 and closed on 26th May 1968, after the remaining freight working ceased. (N.W.Sprinks)

93. We now look east on the same day with ex-GNR class C12 4-4-2T no. 67379 running bunker first with a two-coach train from Essendine, passing the ex-GNR signal box and heading for Stamford East terminus. In the centre are the tracks leading to the stub of the line to Wansford, closed in 1929, and the tracks linking the ex-GNR metals on the left to the ex-Midland metals on the right. (N.W.Sprinks)

94. The map shows the engine shed to be remote from the station, but close to the river and thus near to a water source. Class C12 no. 67376 was recorded on 14th April 1957. The shed was opened on 1st November 1856, extended in 1867 and closed on 15th June 1959. (M.Dart coll.)

95. The ornate railings were added in 1903. The station was closed to passengers on 4th March 1957 and trains were diverted to Town station until 15th June 1959, when the Essendine service ceased. The goods yard was in use until 4th March 1963. The photo is from 9th December 1980. The elegant building survives in residential use. (D.A.Thompson)

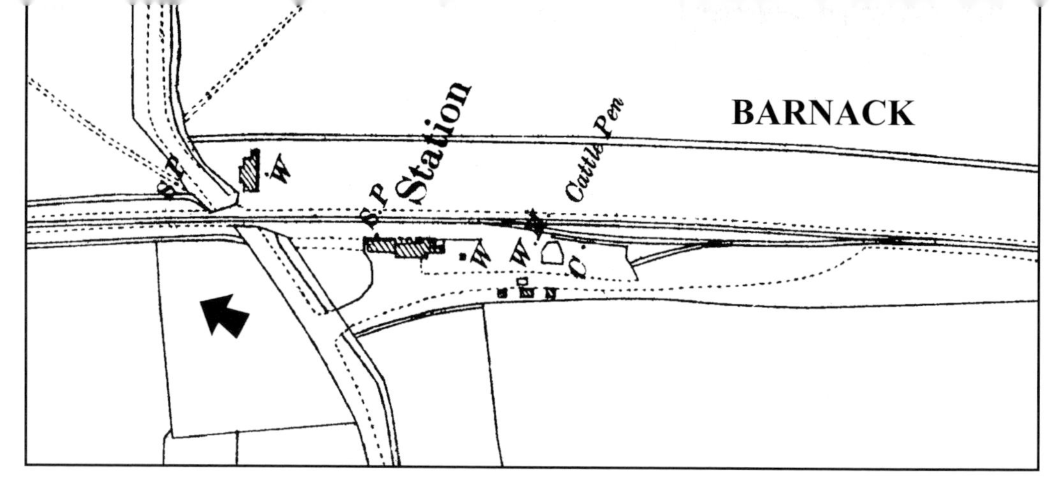

XXXVII. For centuries, the locality produced top quality building stone, but construction of the Houses of Parliament exhausted the supply. Local farmers provided most traffic. The map is from 1900 and includes two wells, marked W, and a weighing machine.

96. The station had two signals and two levers; both of the latter are near this post. Two more were added, when distant signals arrived. Four more came in 1903 to work a new siding. The route was known by some as the 'Bread and Onion Line'. (P.Laming coll.)

97. The local population was 614 in 1901 and 703 in 1961. The goods yard had a crane rated at 1 ton 18cwt when the line opened, but one was not recorded in 1938. Total closure came in 1929, but the building is still standing. (A.Dudman coll.)

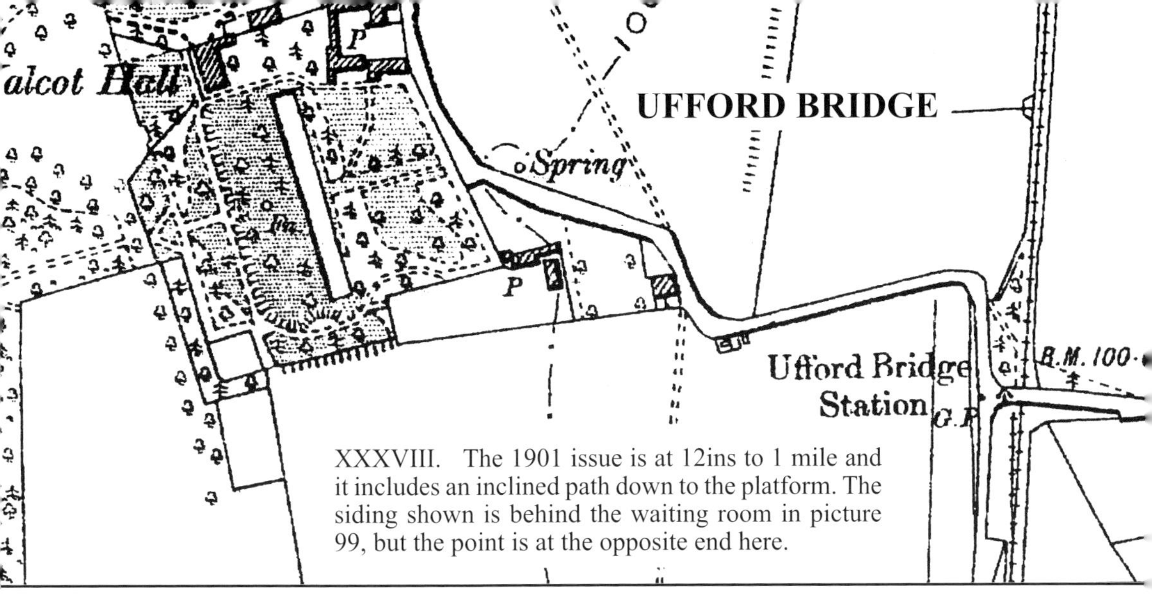

XXXVIII. The 1901 issue is at 12ins to 1 mile and it includes an inclined path down to the platform. The siding shown is behind the waiting room in picture 99, but the point is at the opposite end here.

98. The steps shown were a later addition to the path seen on the map. Until March 1872, trains only called here on Fridays. (Only two in 1867.) The station served the small village of Southorpe, which is in Cambridgeshire, this stretching a mile to the south. (P.Laming coll.)

99. The siding arrived in 1903, together with four levers, but no signals. A siding was added south of here, on the west side, to serve a narrow gauge line carrying materials for the construction of Wittering Airfield, during WWI. (LOSA)

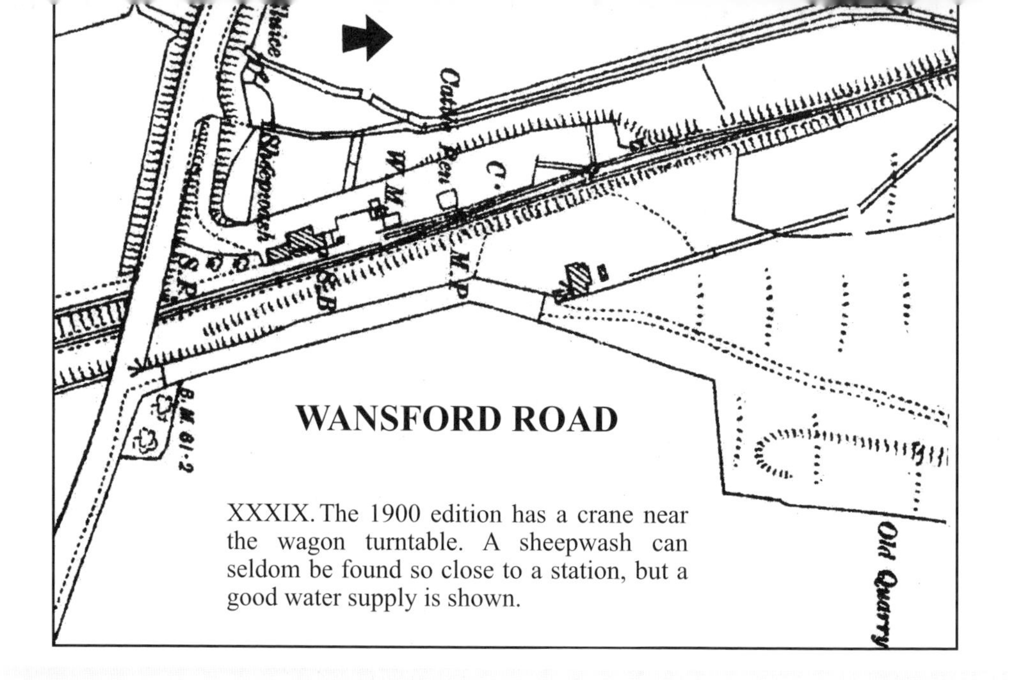

WANSFORD ROAD

XXXIX. The 1900 edition has a crane near the wagon turntable. A sheepwash can seldom be found so close to a station, but a good water supply is shown.

100. A pre-1929 panorama from the bridge includes the crane and loading gauge. The signal box had a 6-lever frame and functioned from 1892 to 1920. (Stations UK)

101. This is the view north from the bridge in 1959, 30 years after the last train had left. It is now a luxury home. There was a station called Sibson, south of here, from 1st January 1870 until 1st March 1878, which was used as a temporary terminus. (R.M.Casserley)

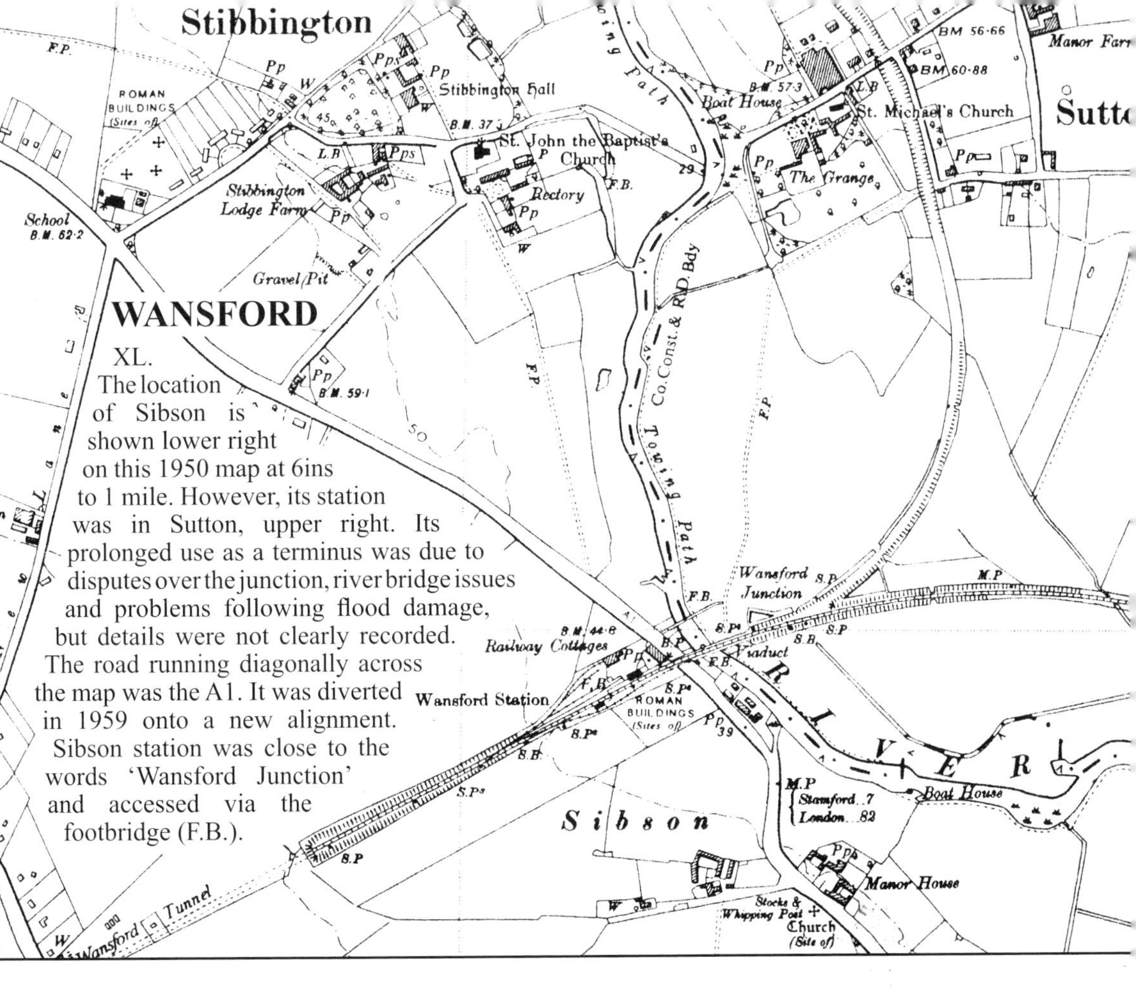

XL. The location of Sibson is shown lower right on this 1950 map at 6ins to 1 mile. However, its station was in Sutton, upper right. Its prolonged use as a terminus was due to disputes over the junction, river bridge issues and problems following flood damage, but details were not clearly recorded. The road running diagonally across the map was the A1. It was diverted in 1959 onto a new alignment. Sibson station was close to the words 'Wansford Junction' and accessed via the footbridge (F.B.).

102. This view west is from about 1900 and at the island platform is GNR no. 630, an 0-4-4T. Two small signal boxes were replaced on 28th April 1907 by the 60-lever one seen in the next picture. The station layout had been improved in 1879, notably by the addition of the third platform. (R.M.Casserley coll.)

See our *Northampton to Peterborough* album for other illustrations. Pictures 69 to 73 show the early era and nos 107 to 111 show the NVR period.

103. There were 408 living in Sibson-cum-Stibbington in 1921. We look towards Peterborough on 29th April 1954, along the London & Birmingham Railway route of 1846. It closed to passengers on 1st July 1957, but reopened on 1st June 1977 as part of the Nene Valley Railway enterprise. A few goods and mineral trains had continued to pass through until 6th November 1972. The box had closed on 30th March 1971, but it remained intact. (H.C.Casserley)

104. The north elevation is seen in 1954. After closure, the building and goods yard were in commercial use until 2016. The NVR then had control of them. The line had been extended west to Yarwell Junction on 7th April 2007, to a new station beyond Wansford Tunnel. (R.M.Casserley coll.)

4. Spalding to Murrow

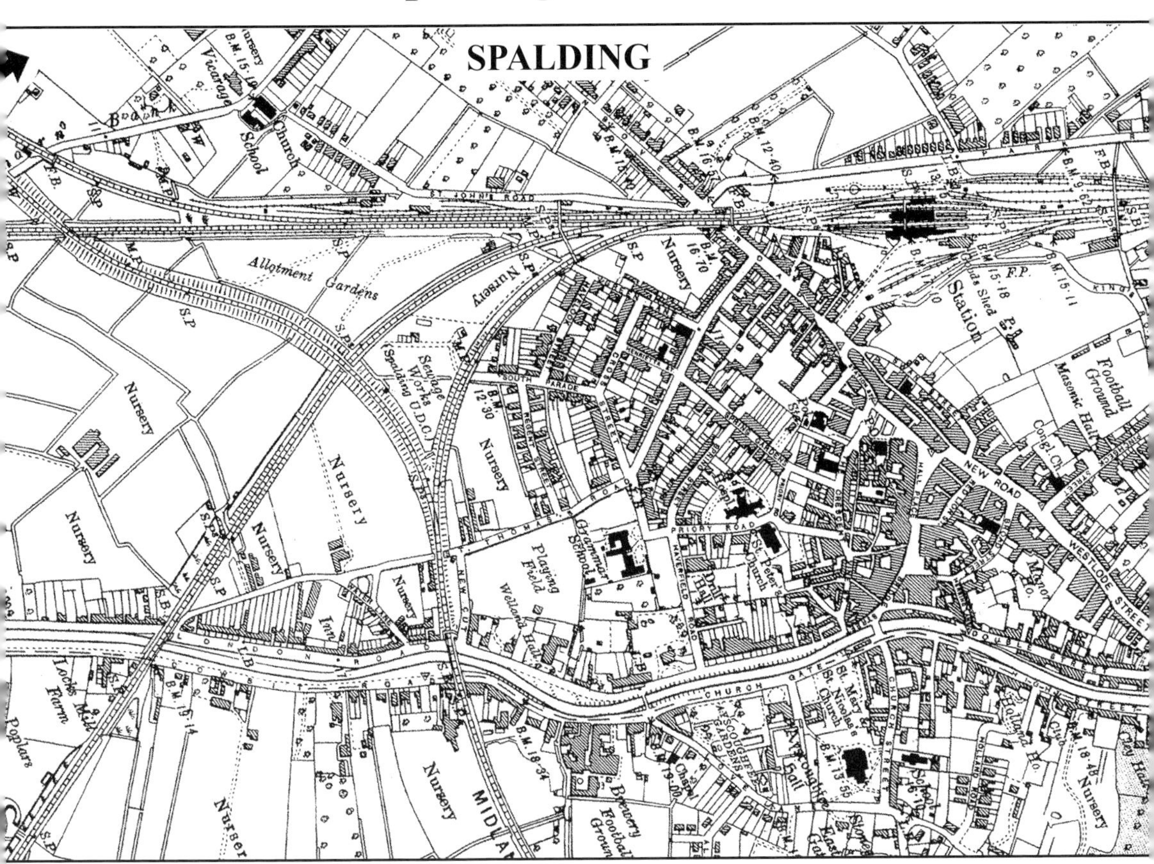

XLIa. The 1932 survey at 6ins to 1 mile has the Peterborough to Boston line from left to right (LNER), the route to Bourne above it on the left (M&GNR), the tracks to Murrow lower left (LNER) and those to South Lynn lower centre (M&GNR).

105. Barrows abound, probably for incoming mail bags, as a train arrives at platform 2. No. 1 is the bay on the right. The platforms were later renumbered simply 1 to 4, starting close to the engine, which cannot be identified. (P.Laming coll.)

106. This 1954 panorama is from platform 6. No. 7 is on the left; they were long used by M&GN trains. No. 5 is on the right. The water tank is beyond the gas lamp. Passenger trains and specials were often loaded with boxes of flowers here. The suffix TOWN was in use from 1948 to 1968. (Stations UK)

XLIb. The 1903 edition at 15ins to 1 mile bears most details of interest, but note the great length of the northern footbridge.

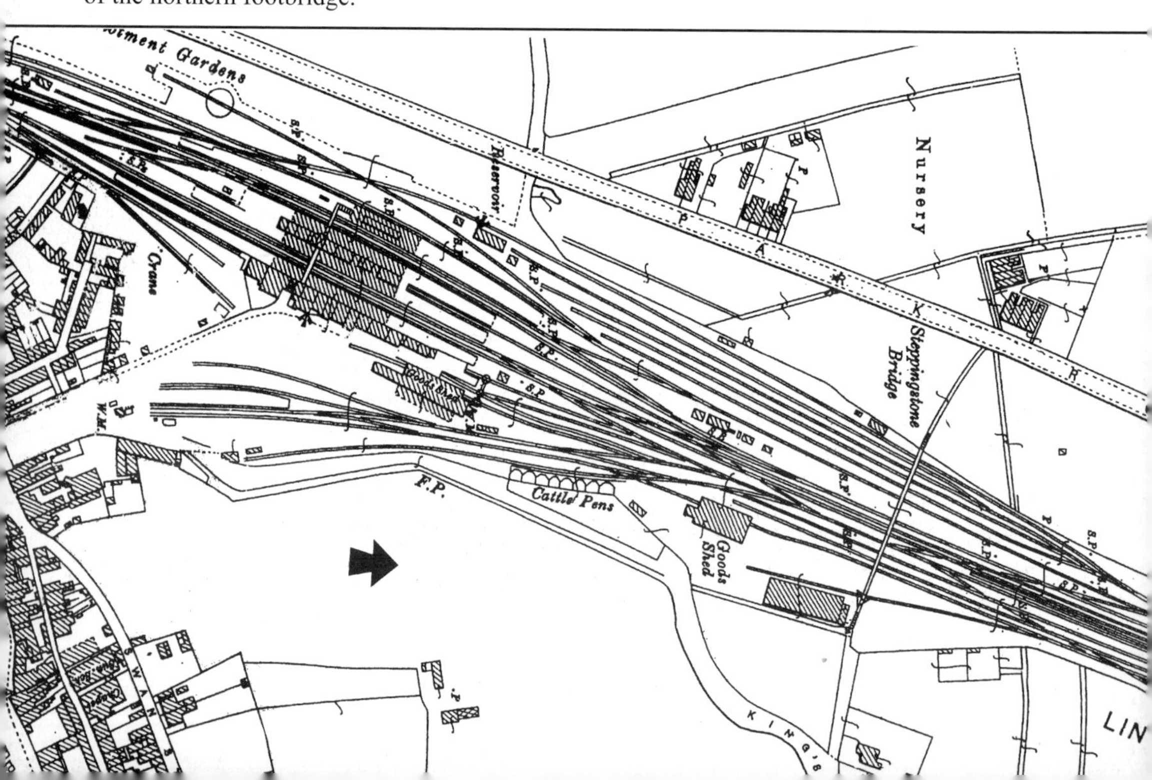

107. Class B17/6 4-6-0 no. 61638 *Melton Hall* approaches with a northbound express in about 1956. Local produce included fruit, cabbages and peas, every day in season. There were just two up and three down passenger trains on Mondays to Fridays in the Summer of 1970. (Milepost 92½)

Other pictures to enjoy are in ***Spalding to Grimsby*** **(pictures 1 to 9),** ***Peterborough to Lincoln*** **(22 to 36) and** ***Branch Lines around Spalding*** **(41 to 50). The first album contains extensive signalling details.**

108. Class V2 2-6-2 no. 60870 is working the 12.54 Doncaster to March on 18th February 1961 and stands at platform 2. Later, special trains carrying visitors to the Spalding Flower Festival became very popular. Around 20 were run on the annual event day in the early 1980s. (E.Wilmshurst)

109. The engine shed and a goods shed are upper left on the first Spalding map, above the Allotment Gardens. The former closed on 7th March 1960. The latter shed was known as St. Johns and it closed on 4th July 1966, being ex-MR. The Spalding-March line closed to all traffic on 27th November 1982. (R.S.Carpenter)

SOUTH OF SPALDING

110. The Welland Bridge is lower left on map XLIa. The 1881 box had 15 levers and closed with the line. This photograph is from 1973. (A.C.Mott)

COWBIT

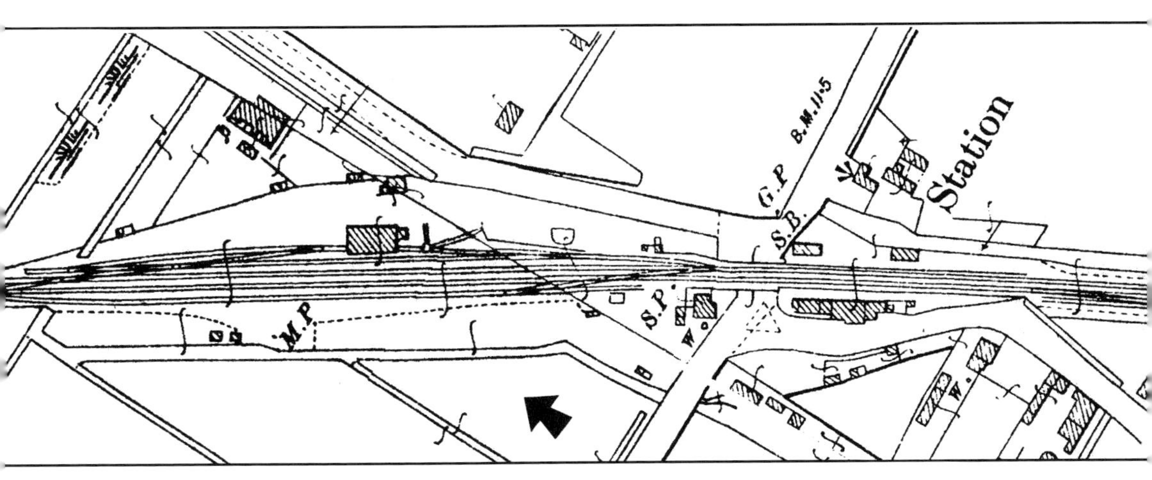

XLII. The village was nearby, to the west. It housed 462 in 1901 and 583 in 1961. It was close to the navigable River Welland. The date is 1903.

111. The stations on the route were all closed to passengers on 11th September 1961. Goods service was retained here until 5th October 1964. This view north is from 11th February 1961. The box had a 35-lever frame and closed with the line. (D.A.Thompson/R.Humm)

112. Running north on 1st July 1981 is no. 40121 with empty stock. A single siding is evident, but all would be gone within two years, except the main buildings. These became part of a residential complex. The final track to be lifted was in the Summer of 1985. The structure on the left became a dog grooming centre, called 'Paws at the Station'. (P.Bevan)

POSTLAND

XLIII. The 1904 edition shows mostly staff dwellings nearby. The others were spread rather widely. The station was called CROWLAND until 1st December 1871.

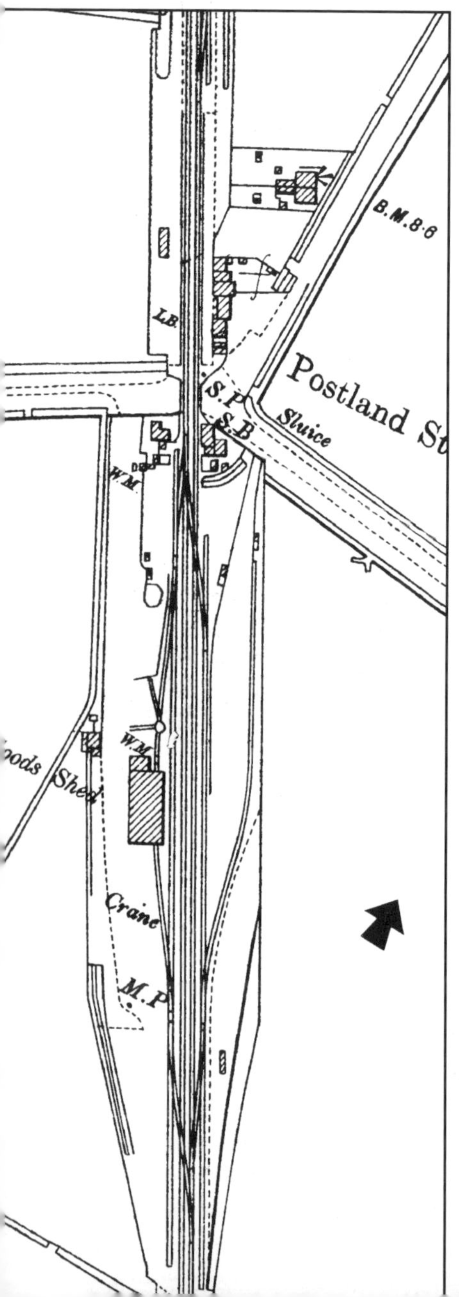

113. We start with two photos from 23rd October 1976. The 1882 box had 36 levers and lasted until the end in 1982. Staff transport was kept safely away from the road. (P.Bevan)

114. Nos E56035 and E50030 pass the goods yard, which had closed on 19th April 1965. The destination is Doncaster. The vans in the other yard are probably stored, awaiting their demise. (P.Bevan)

115. It is 6th September 1980 and a railtour makes a photostop. The Fakenham & Dereham Railway Society titled the trip 'GN/GE Jt. Freight Lines'. It started at March and ran to Wisbech, March, Whitemoor Yard, Spalding, Sleaford, Lincoln, Bardney, Lincoln, Torksey and back to March. All for £5.90. (P.Bevan)

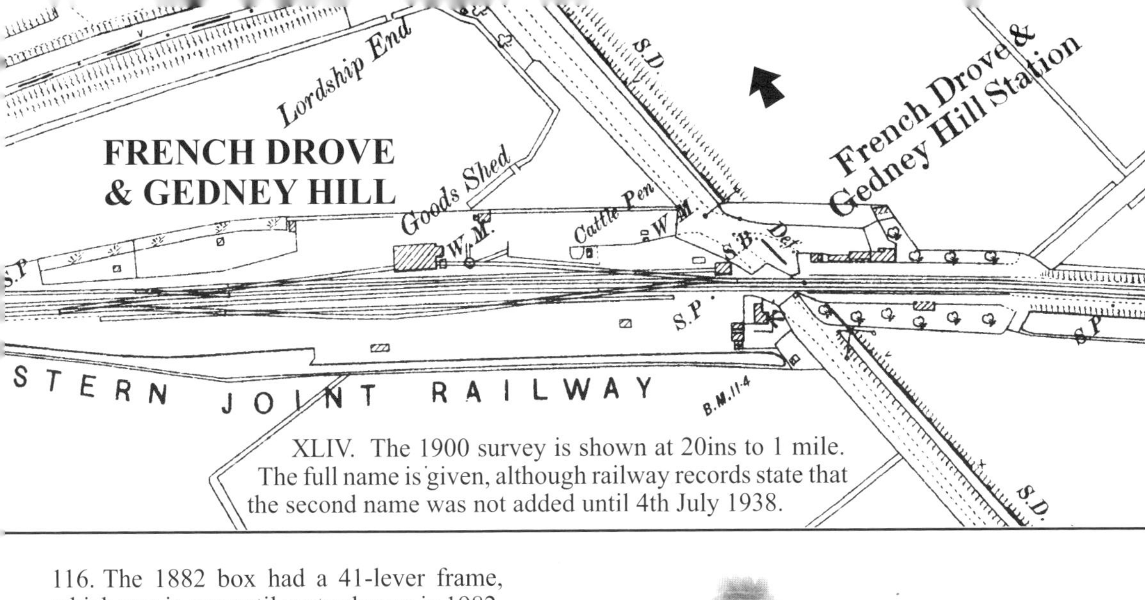

XLIV. The 1900 survey is shown at 20ins to 1 mile. The full name is given, although railway records state that the second name was not added until 4th July 1938.

116. The 1882 box had a 41-lever frame, which was in use until route closure in 1982. Both pictures are from 29th September 1967. The goods yard had been beyond the box until 5th October 1964. (H.C.Casserley)

117. Passenger service was withdrawn on 11th September 1961. It was also lost from 1st January 1917 until 1st February 1919, as a wartime economy measure. Pairs of steam ploughing engines were introduced in the district in that period to improve grain production. No. D5697 is northbound. (H.C.Casserley)

MURROW WEST

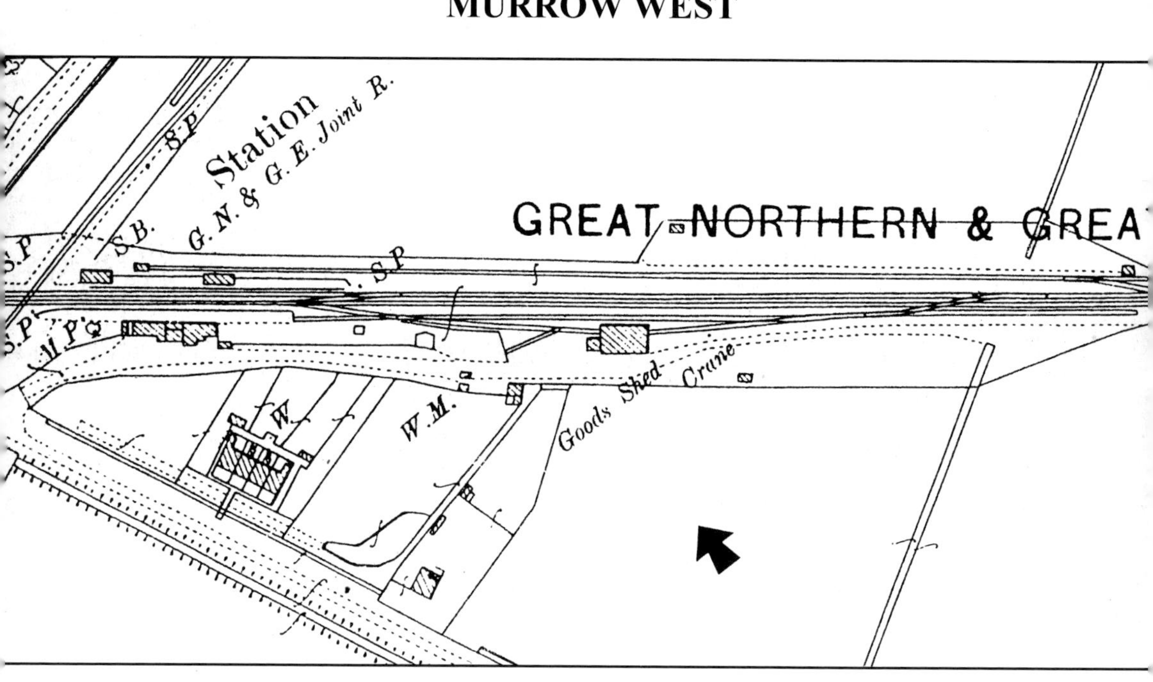

XLV. The 1900 edition has the M&GNR diagonally top left. The goods yard shown closed on 1st September 1947. The term WEST was in use from 27th September 1948 until closure on 6th July 1953.

118. Murrow housed just 979 in 1901, but had two stations, serving all four points of the compass, between them. The M&GN crosses in the foreground. The signal box functioned until 9th October 1941, when it was demolished in an accident and replaced by a temporary hut on 4th November 1941. (LOSA)

Other views of this station are in *Branch Lines around March*, pictures 87 to 89. Murrow East is in *Branch Lines around Wisbech* (33 to 35) and *Peterborough to Kings Lynn* (37 to 44).

119. This view southeast is from 1958. In the distance is the goods shed. The yard was open until 5th October 1964; its crane was rated at 5 tons. On the left is a refuge siding. (D.Rokeby/R.Humm)

120. The replacement signal box opened on 26th November 1950 and is seen on 28th February 1959. A single line curved between the two routes and it came into use on 2nd January 1961. It was situated behind the box and traffic on it continued to Dogsthorpe Brickworks until 1966 and to Wisbech North until 1965. The box eventually became a dwelling. (H.B.Priestley/R.Humm)

MP Middleton Press

EVOLVING THE ULTIMATE RAIL ENCYCLOPEDIA

Easebourne Midhurst GU29 9AZ. Tel:01730 813169

www.middletonpress.co.uk email:info@middletonpress.co.uk
A-978 0 906520 B-978 1 873793 C-978 1 901706 D-978 1 904474
E-978 1 906008 F-978 1 908174

All titles listed below were in print at time of publication - please check current availability by looking at our website - *www.middletonpress.co.uk* or by requesting a Brochure which includes our *LATEST* RAILWAY TITLES also our TRAMWAY, TROLLEYBUS, MILITARY and COASTAL series

A

Abergavenny to Merthyr C 91 8
Abertillery & Ebbw Vale Lines D 84 5
Aberystwyth to Carmarthen E 90 1
Allhallows - Branch Line to A 62 8
Alton - Branch Lines to A 11 6
Andover to Southampton A 82 6
Ascot - Branch Lines around A 64 2
Ashburton - Branch Line to B 95 4
Ashford - Steam to Eurostar B 67 1
Ashford to Dover A 48 2
Austrian Narrow Gauge D 04 3
Avonmouth - BL around D 42 5
Aylesbury to Rugby D 91 3

B

Baker Street to Uxbridge D 90 6
Bala to Llandudno E 87 1
Banbury to Birmingham D 27 2
Banbury to Cheltenham E 63 5
Bangor to Holyhead F 01 7
Bangor to Portmadoc E 72 7
Barking to Southend C 80 2
Barmouth to Pwllheli E 53 6
Barry - Branch Lines around D 50 0
Bartlow - Branch Lines to F 27 7
Bath Green Park to Bristol C 36 9
Bath to Evercreech Junction A 60 4
Beamish 40 years on rails E94 9
Bedford to Wellingborough D 31 9
Berwick to Drem F 64 2
Berwick to St. Boswells F 75 8
B'ham to Tamworth & Nuneaton F 63 5
Birkenhead to West Kirby F 61 1
Birmingham to Wolverhampton E253
Blackburn to Hellifield F 95 6
Bletchley to Cambridge D 94 4
Bletchley to Rugby E 07 9
Bodmin - Branch Lines around B 83 1
Boston to Lincoln F 80 2
Bournemouth to Evercreech Jn A 46 8
Bournemouth to Weymouth A 57 4
Bradshaw's History F18 5
Bradshaw's Rail Times 1850 F 13 0
Bradshaw's Rail Times 1895 F 11 6
Branch Lines series - see town names
Brecon to Neath D 43 2
Brecon to Newport D 16 6
Brecon to Newtown E 06 2
Brighton to Eastbourne A 16 1
Brighton to Worthing A 03 1
Bristol to Taunton D 03 6
Bromley South to Rochester B 23 7
Bromsgrove to Birmingham D 87 6
Bromsgrove to Gloucester D 73 9
Broxbourne to Cambridge F16 1
Brunel - A railtour D 74 6
Bude - Branch Line to B 29 9
Burnham to Evercreech Jn B 68 0

C

Cambridge to Ely D 55 5
Canterbury - BLs around B 58 9
Cardiff to Dowlais (Cae Harris) E 47 5
Cardiff to Pontypridd E 95 6
Cardiff to Swansea E 42 0
Carlisle to Hawick E 85 7
Carmarthen to Fishguard E 66 6
Caterham & Tattenham Corner B251
Central & Southern Spain NG E 91 8
Chard and Yeovil - BLs a C 30 7
Charing Cross to Dartford A 75 8
Charing Cross to Orpington A 96 3
Cheddar - Branch Line to B 90 9
Cheltenham to Andover C 43 7
Cheltenham to Redditch D 81 4
Chester to Birkenhead F 21 5
Chester to Manchester F 51 2
Chester to Rhyl E 93 2
Chester to Warrington F 40 6
Chichester to Portsmouth A 14 7
Clacton and Walton - BLs to F 04 8
Clapham Jn to Beckenham Jn B 36 7
Cleobury Mortimer - BLs a E 18 5
Clevedon & Portishead - BLs to D180
Consett to South Shields E 57 4
Cornwall Narrow Gauge D 56 2
Corris and Vale of Rheidol E 65 9
Craven Arms to Llandeilo E 35 2
Craven Arms to Wellington E 33 8
Crawley to Littlehampton A 34 5
Crewe to Manchester F 57 4
Cromer - Branch Lines around C 26 0
Croydon to East Grinstead B 48 0
Crystal Palace & Catford Loop B 87 1
Cyprus Narrow Gauge E 13 0

D

Darjeeling Revisited F 09 3
Darlington Leamside Newcastle E 28 4
Darlington to Newcastle D 98 2
Dartford to Sittingbourne B 34 3
Denbigh - Branch Lines around F 32 1
Derby to Stoke-on-Trent F 93 2
Derwent Valley - BL to the D 06 7
Devon Narrow Gauge E 09 3
Didcot to Banbury D 02 9
Didcot to Swindon C 84 0
Didcot to Winchester C 13 0
Dorset & Somerset NG D 76 0
Douglas - Laxey - Ramsey E 75 8
Douglas to Peel C 88 8
Douglas to Port Erin C 55 0
Douglas to Ramsey D 39 5
Dover to Ramsgate A 78 9
Dublin Northwards in 1950s E 31 4
Dunstable - Branch Lines to E 27 7

E

Ealing to Slough C 42 0
Eastbourne to Hastings A 27 7
East Cornwall Mineral Railways D 22 7
East Croydon to Three Bridges A 53 6
Eastern Spain Narrow Gauge E 56 7
East Grinstead - BLs to A 07 9
East Kent Light Railway A 61 1
East London - Branch Lines of C 44 4
East London Line B 80 0
East of Norwich - Branch Lines E 69 7
Effingham Junction - BLs a A 74 1
Ely to Norwich C 90 1
Enfield Town & Palace Gates D 32 6
Epsom to Horsham A 30 7
Eritrean Narrow Gauge E 38 3
Euston to Harrow & Wealdstone C 89 5
Exeter to Barnstaple B 15 2
Exeter to Newton Abbot C 49 9
Exeter to Tavistock B 69 5
Exmouth - Branch Lines to B 00 8

F

Fairford - Branch Line to A 52 9
Falmouth, Helston & St. Ives C 74 1
Fareham to Salisbury A 67 3
Faversham to Dover B 05 3
Felixstowe & Aldeburgh - BL to D 20 3
Fenchurch Street to Barking C 20 8
Festiniog - 50 yrs of enterprise C 83 3
Festiniog 1946-55 E 01 7
Festiniog in the Fifties B 68 8
Festiniog in the Sixties B 91 6
Ffestiniog in Colour 1955-82 F 25 3
Finsbury Park to Alexandra Pal C 02 8
French Metre Gauge Survivors F 88 8
Frome to Bristol B 77 0

G

Galashiels to Edinburgh F 52 9
Gloucester to Bristol D 35 7
Gloucester to Cardiff D 66 1
Gosport - Branch Lines around A 36 9
Greece Narrow Gauge D 72 2

H

Hampshire Narrow Gauge D 36 4
Harrow to Watford D 14 2
Harwich & Hadleigh - BLs to F 02 4
Harz Revisited F 62 8
Hastings to Ashford A 37 6
Hawick to Galashiels F 36 9
Hawkhurst - Branch Line to A 66 6
Hayling - Branch Line to A 12 3
Hay-on-Wye - BL around D 92 0
Haywards Heath to Seaford A 28 4
Hemel Hempstead - BLs to D 88 3
Henley, Windsor & Marlow - BLa C77 2
Hereford to Newport D 54 8
Hertford & Hatfield - BLs a E 58 1
Hertford Loop E 71 0
Hexham to Carlisle D 75 3
Hexham to Hawick F 08 6
Hitchin to Peterborough D 07 4
Holborn Viaduct to Lewisham A 81 9
Horsham - Branch Lines to A 02 4
Huntingdon - Branch Line to A 93 2

I

Ilford to Shenfield C 97 0
Ilfracombe - Branch Line to B 21 3
Industrial Rlys of the South East A 09 3
Ipswich to Diss F 81 9
Ipswich to Saxmundham C 41 3
Isle of Wight Lines - 50 yrs C 12 3
Italy Narrow Gauge F 17 8

K

Kent Narrow Gauge C 45 1
Kettering to Nottingham F 82-6
Kidderminster to Shrewsbury E 10 9
Kingsbridge - Branch Line to C 98 7
Kings Cross to Potters Bar E 62 8
King's Lynn to Hunstanton F 58 1
Kingston & Hounslow Loops A 83 3
Kingswear - Branch Line to C 17 8

L

Lambourn - Branch Line to C 70 3
Launceston & Princetown - BLs C 19 2
Leicester to Burton F 85 7
Lewisham to Dartford A 92 5
Lincoln to Cleethorpes F 56 7
Lines around Stamford F 98 7
Lines around Wimbledon B 75 6
Liverpool Street to Chingford D 01 2
Liverpool Street to Ilford C 34 5
Llandeilo to Swansea E 46 8
London Bridge to Addiscombe B 20 6
London Bridge to East Croydon A 58 1
Longmoor - Branch Lines to A 41 3
Looe - Branch Line to C 22 2
Loughborough to Nottingham F 68 0
Lowestoft - BLs around E 40 6
Ludlow to Hereford E 14 7
Lydney - Branch Lines around E 26 0
Lyme Regis - Branch Line to A 45 1
Lynton - Branch Line to B 04 6

M

Machynlleth to Barmouth E 54 3
Maesteg and Tondu Lines E 06 2
Majorca & Corsica Narrow Gauge F 41 3
March - Branch Lines around B 09 1
Market Drayton - BLs around F 67 3
Market Harborough to Newark F 86 4
Marylebone to Rickmansworth D 49 4
Melton Constable to Yarmouth Bch E031
Midhurst - Branch Lines of E 78 9
Midhurst - Branch Lines to F 00 0
Minehead - Branch Line to A 80 2
Mitcham Junction Lines B 01 5
Monmouth - Branch Lines to E 20 8
Monmouthshire Eastern Valleys D 71 5
Moretonhampstead - BL to C 27 7
Moreton-in-Marsh to Worcester D 26 5
Morpeth to Bellingham F 87 1
Mountain Ash to Neath D 80 7

N

Newark to Doncaster F 78 9
Newbury to Westbury C 66 6
Newcastle to Hexham D 69 2
Newport (IOW) - Branch Lines to A 26 0
Newquay - Branch Lines to C 71 0
Newton Abbot to Plymouth C 60 4
Newtown to Aberystwyth E 41 3
Northampton to Peterborough F 92 5
North East German NG D 44 9
Northern Alpine Narrow Gauge F 37 6
Northern France Narrow Gauge C 75 8
Northern Spain Narrow Gauge E 83 3
North London Line B 94 7
North of Birmingham F 55 0
North Woolwich - BLs around C 65 9
Nottingham to Boston F 70 3
Nottingham to Lincoln F 43 7

O

Ongar - Branch Line to E 05 5
Orpington to Tonbridge B 03 9
Oswestry - Branch Lines around E 60 4
Oswestry to Whitchurch E 81 9
Oxford to Bletchley D 57 9
Oxford to Moreton-in-Marsh D 15 9

P

Paddington to Ealing C 37 6
Paddington to Princes Risborough C819
Padstow - Branch Line to B 54 1
Pembroke and Cardigan - BLs to F 29 1
Peterborough to Kings Lynn E 32 1
Peterborough to Lincoln F 89 5
Peterborough to Newark F 72 7
Plymouth - BLs around B 98 5
Plymouth to St. Austell C 63 5
Pontypool to Mountain Ash D 65 4
Pontypridd to Merthyr F 14 7
Pontypridd to Port Talbot E 86 4
Porthmadog 1954-94 - BLa B 31 2
Portmadoc 1923-46 - BLa B 13 8
Portsmouth to Southampton A 31 4
Portugal Narrow Gauge E 67 3
Potters Bar to Cambridge D 70 8
Princes Risborough - BL to D 05 0
Princes Risborough to Banbury C 85 7

R

Railways to Victory C 16 1
Reading to Basingstoke B 27 5
Reading to Didcot C 79 6
Reading to Guildford A 47 5
Redhill to Ashford A 73 4
Return to Blaenau 1970-82 C 64 2
Rhyl to Bangor F 15 4
Rhymney & New Tredegar Lines E 48 2
Rickmansworth to Aylesbury D 61 6
Romania & Bulgaria NG E 23 9
Romneyrail C 32 1
Ross-on-Wye - BLs around E 30 7
Ruabon to Barmouth E 84 0
Rugby to Birmingham E 37 6
Rugby to Loughborough F 12 3
Rugby to Stafford F 07 9
Rugeley to Stoke-on-Trent F 90 1
Ryde to Ventnor A 19 2

S

Salisbury to Westbury B 39 8
Sardinia and Sicily Narrow Gauge F 50 5
Saxmundham to Yarmouth C 69 7
Saxony & Baltic Germany Revisited F 71 0
Saxony Narrow Gauge D 47 0
Seaton & Sidmouth - BLs to A 95 6
Selsey - Branch Line to A 04 8
Sheerness - Branch Line to B 16 2
Shenfield to Ipswich E 96 3
Shrewsbury - Branch Line to A 86 4
Shrewsbury to Chester E 70 3
Shrewsbury to Crewe F 48 2
Shrewsbury to Ludlow E 21 5
Shrewsbury to Newtown E 29 1
Sierra Leone Narrow Gauge D 28 9
Sirhowy Valley Line E 12 3
Sittingbourne to Ramsgate A 90 1
Skegness & Mablethorpe - BL to F 84 0
Slough to Newbury C 56 7
South African Two-foot gauge E 51 2
Southampton to Bournemouth A 42 0
Southend & Southminster BLs E 76 5
Southern Alpine Narrow Gauge F 22 2
Southern France Narrow Gauge C 47 5
South London Line B 46 6
South Lynn to Norwich City F 03 1
Southwold - Branch Line to A 15 4
Spalding - Branch Lines around E 52 9
Spalding to Grimsby F 65 9 6
Stafford to Chester F 34 5
Stafford to Wellington F 59 8
St Albans to Bedford D 08 1
St. Austell to Penzance C 67 3
St. Boswell to Berwick F 44 4
Steaming Through Isle of Wigh
Steaming Through West Hants
Stourbridge to Wolverhampton
St. Pancras to Barking D 68 5
St. Pancras to Folkestone E 88
St. Pancras to St. Albans C 78
Stratford to Cheshunt F 53 6
Stratford-u-Avon to Birmingha
Stratford-u-Avon to Cheltenha
Sudbury - Branch Lines to F 1
Surrey Narrow Gauge C 87 1
Sussex Narrow Gauge C 68 0
Swaffham - Branch Lines arou
Swanage to 1999 - BL to A 33
Swanley to Ashford B 45 9
Swansea - Branch Lines arour
Swansea to Carmarthen E 59
Swindon to Bristol C 96 3
Swindon to Gloucester D 46 3
Swindon to Newport D 30 2
Swiss Narrow Gauge C 94 9

T

Talyllyn 60 E 98 7
Tamworth to Derby F 76 5
Taunton to Barnstaple B 60 2
Taunton to Exeter C 82 6
Taunton to Minehead F 39 0
Tavistock to Plymouth B 88 6
Tenterden - Branch Line to A 2
Three Bridges to Brighton A 35
Tilbury Loop C 86 4
Tiverton - BLs around C 62 8
Tivetshall to Beccles D 41 8
Tonbridge to Hastings A 44 4
Torrington - Branch Lines to B
Towcester - BLs around E 39 0
Tunbridge Wells BLs A 32 1

U

Upwell - Branch Line to B 64 0

V

Victoria to Bromley South A 98
Victoria to East Croydon A 40
Vivarais Revisited E 08 6

W

Walsall Routes F 45 1
Wantage - Branch Line to D 25
Wareham to Swanage 50 yrs D
Waterloo to Windsor A 54 3
Waterloo to Woking A 38 3
Watford to Leighton Buzzard D
Wellingborough to Leicester F
Welshpool to Llanfair E 49 9
Wenford Bridge to Fowey C 09
Westbury to Bath B 55 8
Westbury to Taunton C 76 5
West Cornwall Mineral Rlys D
West Croydon to Epsom B 08
West German Narrow Gauge D
West London - BLs of C 50 5
West London Line B 84 8
West Wiltshire - BLs of D 12 8
Weymouth - BLs A 65 9
Willesden Jn to Richmond B 7
Wimbledon to Beckenham C 5
Wimbledon to Epsom B 62 6
Wimborne - BLs around A 97
Wisbech - BLs around C 01 7
Witham & Kelvedon - BLs a E
Woking to Alton A 59 8
Woking to Portsmouth A 25 3
Woking to Southampton A 55
Wolverhampton to Shrewsbury
Wolverhampton to Stafford F 7
Worcester to Birmingham D 97
Worcester to Hereford D 38 8
Worthing to Chichester A 06 2
Wrexham to New Brighton F 47
Wroxham - BLs around F 31 4

Y

Yeovil - 50 yrs change C 38 3
Yeovil to Dorchester A 76 5
Yeovil to Exeter A 91 8
York to Scarborough F 23 9